SALARY SUCCESS

Other books by Drs. Ron and Caryl Krannich

The Almanac of American Government Jobs and Careers
The Almanac of International Jobs and Careers
Careering and Re-Careering for the 1990s
The Complete Guide to International Jobs and Careers
The Complete Guide to Public Employment
Discover the Right Job for You!
The Educator's Guide to Alternative Jobs and Careers
Find a Federal Job Fast!
High Impact Resumes and Letters (with William Banis)
Interview for Success
Mayors and Managers
Moving Out of Education (with William Banis)
Moving Out of Government
Network Your Way to Job and Career Success
The Politics of Family Planning Policy
Re-Careering in Turbulent Times
Shopping in Exciting Australia and Papua New Guinea
Shopping in Exotic Asia
Shopping in Exotic Hong Kong (with Jo Reimer)
Shopping in Exotic Indonesia
Shopping in Exotic Places (with Jo Reimer)
Shopping in Exotic Singapore and Malaysia
Shopping in Exotic Thailand
Shopping in the Exotic Philippines
Shopping the Exotic South Pacific

SALARY SUCCESS

Ronald L. Krannich, Ph.D.
Caryl Rae Krannich, Ph.D.

IMPACT PUBLICATIONS
Woodbridge, VA

SALARY SUCCESS: Know What You're Worth and Get It!

Library of Congress Cataloguing-in-Publication Data

Krannich, Ronald L.
    Salary success / Ronald L. Krannich. Caryl Rae Krannich.
      p. cm.
    Includes bibliographical references (p.   ) and index.
    ISBN 0-942710-34-7 (hardback) : $22.95.
    ISBN 0-942710-35-5 (pbk.) : $11.95
    1. Applications for positions. 2. Wages. I. Krannich, Caryl
Rae. II. Title.
HF5383.K72 1990   90-4945
650.1'2--dc20   CIP

For information on distribution or quantity discount rates, Tel. 703/361-7300, FAX 703/335-9486, or write to: Sales Department, IMPACT PUBLICATIONS, 4580 Sunshine Court, Woodbridge, VA 22192. Distributed to the trade by National Book Network, 4720 Boston Way, Suite A, Lanham, MD 20706, Tel. 301/459-8696.

CONTENTS

PREFACE

Few job related activities are so important yet so neglected as salary negotiations. While individuals may do well in learning how to find and do a job, they often fail to negotiate an appropriate salary figure that accurately reflects their qualifications for the job and value to employers. Thinking that salaries are largely predetermined, or feeling uncomfortable talking about money to employers, they accept the first salary offered to them. Yet, the salary they accept today will become a powerful determiner of future salary increases.

We wrote this book because we saw a need to approach this subject in a more systematic manner than heretofore attempted. Indeed, numerous myths and mistakes prevent job seekers and employees from taking effective salary action that could translate into thousands of dollars in additional income. Taking compensation as our major focus, we outline the key issues and strategies that are central to valuing positions as well as individuals within organizations. We examine the salary logic of both employers and employees in the process of reaching agreement on valuing positions and individual performance. The result is a book that puts *individual performance* rather than clever negotiating tactics at the center of any discussion concerning salary and benefits. As such, the book should be useful to job seekers, employees, and employers alike who share similar values in the workplace.

If you are first entering the job market, changing jobs, or advancing your career within an organization, you need to directly deal with the question of salary early in your job search as well as on the job. Contrary to what you may think, salary is not something to be left solely to the discretion of employers. It's an issue that involves important *communication*. From the very beginning of a job search to when you leave the workforce, you need to continuously communicate your qualifications and performance to employers who have the power to dispense rewards.

Whether we like to admit it or not, money is important to us and those we work with. In addition to making life more convenient, it helps us *keep score* on how we are doing in comparison to others. How much we make tells us something about how others value our skills and abilities. At the very least, you should try to get as high a score as possible with your present and future employers.

The chapters that follow are designed to help you improve your salary score and better keep score for many years to come. If you begin by focusing on what benefits you can give employers – rather than what benefits employers can give to you – you will take a major step in the right direction for improving your future salaries.

When performance meets money, expect money to talk seriously about rewarding performance with a better than average salary figure. If, as we outline in this book, you can get money to talk about performance, you will be well on your way to achieving salary success!

                                        Ronald L. Krannich
                                        Caryl Rae Krannich

Chapter One

THE SALARY GAME

What are you worth, and how can you get top dollar in today's job market? This two-part question remains a central concern for many job seekers and employees who believe they may accept a salary that is beneath their true value and who feel uncomfortable dealing with wage and benefit issues. Indeed, most people are probably under-compensated by 10 to 25 percent, because they fail to estimate their worth as well as properly negotiate the highest possible salary. Since the salary you accept today will largely determine your salary tomorrow, over a 10 to 20 year period you may be underpaid by more than $100,000!

LET'S TALK MONEY

In American culture we are taught not to ask other people about how much they make. That would be rude, impolite, and insensitive. What you make is your own business — and your employer's business. It's a secret everyone tries to keep, but one everyone would like to uncover about others. It's the subject of gossip, rumors, leaks, organizational politics, envy, and backbiting.

1

Surprisingly, we do a very good job of keeping our salaries and incomes secret from our colleagues, co-workers, friends, neighbors, and even family members. Only you, your employer, the IRS, and perhaps your mortgage company really know how much you make. In the meantime, we guess about incomes through such superficial visual cues as the size and quality of people's homes, cars, dress, lifestyles, and other worldly possessions.

How, then, do you know what you're really worth in a society which doesn't readily share salary information? And if you don't know what other's make where you work, how will you know if you are being fairly compensated? We know it's not a good idea to directly approach someone and ask them *"What do you make?"* While this question is quite acceptable in many other cultures, it doesn't go down well in American culture. Such a question makes others feel uncomfortable as well as brands you as someone who is rude and nosy. After all, most people try to avoid rude and nosy people.

But there are other ways to get at the salary question. Every year, for example, numerous salary surveys are published on who makes what. While some of these surveys primarily focus on the salaries of Fortune 500 executives who make $400,000 or more each year, other surveys cover a wide range of jobs. Unfortunately, most of these surveys generalize for the nation as a whole rather than identify differences amongst regions. Architects in New York City, for example, make a lot more money than architects in Peoria, Illinois or Billings, Montana.

Government employees and teachers are probably the most well informed about salaries. They know where they and many of their co-workers fit on the official salary schedule. Their major concern is with annual salary increments as well as the comparability of their *"public service"* salaries to private sector salaries. Therefore, the government periodically conducts *"comparability"* studies to identify how much government salaries lag behind those in the private sector. Teachers prefer to compare the salaries they receive in their school district or institution with salaries offered in other school districts or institutions. In so doing, they learn how much they are worth given the *"going rates"* found elsewhere. The concept of *"comparable worth"* that generates comparative salary surveys will usually give them a fairly accurate estimate of how much they should make, give or take a few thousand dollars.

GETTING HIRED HIGHER

But knowing what others make is no guarantee that you will make the same. In fact, you may quickly discover the salary averages are nothing more than the summary of large ranges. For example, an average salary of $43,000 a year for an administrative assistant position may mask the fact that the real range for the job is actually $17,000 to $95,000 a year. Knowing that the average is $43,000 may not help you when you are offered $21,000 a year!

In addition to knowing what others make, we also need to know what you and the job are worth as well as how to best respond to initial salary offers that may be beneath our expectations. The processes of *"valuing"* jobs and your capabilities and communicating this value to employers involves researching jobs, positions, and organizations and developing effective interview and salary negotiation skills. The linking of information to these special job search and salary negotiation skills is what this book is all about.

Most people are under-compensated, because they do not adequately deal with the salary question.

THE PROBLEM WITH SALARIES

Most people are under-compensated, because they do not adequately deal with the salary question. Indeed, many applicants are excellent at writing resumes and conducting job interviews, but they fidget and fumble when asked about salary. Many just take what is offered, because they believe that is all there is, the job is worth what's being offered, or they feel uncomfortable talking about money. They also believe what employers tell them about salaries – they can only pay what is budgeted for the position and the *"going rate"*. Most importantly, they are not *prepared* to deal with the question of compensation because they:

1. Don't know what they or their jobs are worth.

2. Don't know how to effectively negotiate salaries.

3. Believe what employers tell them about salaries.

4. Focus on the wrong issues relevant to compensation.

5. Say the wrong things at the wrong time.

6. Fail to continuously communicate as well as demonstrate their value on resumes, in job interviews, and on the job.

In other words, they are prone to making numerous *mistakes* about what they should be paid. Repeating these mistakes many times over their worklife, they literally lose thousands of dollars in potential earnings.

Salary should become the central focus around which both you and the employer assign value to the job and your performance.

YOUR GUIDE TO SALARY SUCCESS

Most people can improve their ability to address the question of compensation by both learning what they and the job are worth and acquiring some basic salary negotiation skills. By linking comparative salary information to particular jobs and employers, they should be able to negotiate higher salaries. At the same time, they will better demonstrate their value and competence to employers by addressing the salary question within the context of their performance and capabilities.

Rather than relegate salary to the category of something you would rather not talk about, the issue of salary should become the central focus around which both you and the employer assign *value* to the job and your performance. By focusing intelligently on salary and compensation, both you and the employer better define the job and your position within the organization.

That is the purpose of this book – showing you how to value your worth and get the best salary possible. Our concern here is not with *"winning"* any so-called salary game through positive thinking, gamesmanship, manipulation, or clever negotiation skills. Instead, our concern is with *communication* – how to best communicate your qualifications, value, benefits, and performance to employers in exchange for status, position, money, and extras.

Since communications should be a two-way exchange of information, we also are concerned with how employers can best communicate the value of their organization, positions, and jobs to you. Put another way, we want you to locate jobs that are at your best level of capabilities and communicate your value to employers in the most favorable financial terms possible. If you can do this, you will indeed achieve salary success. For in the end, you will do both the employer and yourself -- as well as the job and organization -- a favor by addressing this salary question head-on with information and demonstrated capabilities.

A DIFFERENT APPROACH

Our approach to this subject is different from other examinations of salaries. First, we place the salary question within the larger *context* of the job search, employers, and organizations. An important principle operates here: good salary negotiation skills are based on a firm job search foundation involving knowledge of what you do well and enjoy doing -- your strengths, values, goals -- in order to be better able to communicate your value to employers. This is much more than just another *"you can negotiate anything"* game. It is first and foremost a *process of communicating value* from start to finish in a job search as well as on the job. For in the end, how well you negotiate your salary may determine how well you get along with the employer and your job.

Second, to be most successful in addressing the salary question, we believe you need both information and skills. The *information* comes in two forms:

1. Information about salary issues and negotiations.

2. Information on comparable salary ranges relevant to the jobs you seek.

Therefore, the first 10 chapters of this book address salary issues and the salary negotiation process. Chapter Eleven examines key resources for determining salary ranges. While some readers will find the first 10 chapters most useful, others will be primarily oriented to the information in Chapter Eleven. However, we believe you need to relate both pieces of information in order to be most effective in addressing the salary question.

Good salary negotiation skills are based on a firm job search foundation involving knowledge of what you do well and enjoy doing.

The *skills* you need are primarily communication skills. They focus on gathering and exchanging information about you, the employer, the job, and the organization both during your job search and on the job. Our emphasis here is on developing a very important skill that you will continuously use throughout your worklife rather than on a transitory skill that is only used during a 30-minute salary negotiation period once every five years. This is a long-term capability that hopefully you will use again and again in the process of continually communicating your value to employers and then translating that value into even higher salaries. This *"salary success skill"* should become for you what the performance appraisal skill is for employers. Better still, your salary skill should be aimed at incorporating the employer's performance appraisal in the process of determining compensation.

ACQUIRE USEFUL RESOURCES

Each year millions of job hunters turn to career planning books for assistance. Normally they begin with a general book and next turn to resume and interview books. They may also find a few books, such as this one, that provide information on specific steps in the job search and employment processes.

If this book represents your first career book, you may want to supplement it with a few other key books. When we discuss the importance of resumes, networking, and interviewing, for example, we recommend that you consult separate detailed volumes such as *High Impact Resumes and Letters, Network Your Way to Job and Career Success* and *Interview for Success* that show you how to effectively complete each of these job search steps. These and many other books are available in your local library and bookstore, or they can be ordered directly from Impact Publications by completing the order form at the end of this book.

As a user of this book, you are entitled to a free copy of the most comprehensive career catalog available today -- *"Jobs and Careers for the 1990s"*. To receive the latest edition of this catalog of nearly 1,000 annotated career resources, simply write, fax, or call:

IMPACT PUBLICATIONS
ATTN: Careers Catalog
4580 Sunshine Court
Woodbridge, VA 22192
Tel. 703/361-7300
FAX 703/335-9486

They will send you a copy immediately upon request. Their catalog contains almost every important career and job finding resource available today, including many titles that are difficult if not impossible to find in bookstores and libraries. Included in this catalog are 11 of our other career planning and job search titles that examine other critical steps in the job search process as well as careers in special employment fields: *The Almanac of American Government Jobs and Careers, The Complete Guide to Public Employment, Find a Federal Job Fast!, The Complete Guide to International Jobs and Careers, The Almanac of International Jobs and Careers, Careering and Re-Careering for the 1990s, High Impact*

Resumes and Letters, Interview for Success, Network Your Way to Job and Career Success, Discover the Right Job for You, and *The Educator's Guide to Alternative Jobs and Careers.* You will also find a few other books on salaries and the salary negotiation process which may help supplement or reinforce the information found in this book.

Chapter Two

MYTHS, MISTAKES, AND MONEY IN YOUR FUTURE

Few people are prepared to effectively deal with the money question during job interviews as well as on the job. Part of the problem is how they view themselves, jobs, employers, and issues relating to money. They believe in many myths that prevent them from taking effective salary action. These myths, in turn, lead to many mistakes relating to the money question. And these mistakes tend to under-value many peoples' true value in today's job market.

MYTHS AND REALITIES

MYTH 1: *Since salaries are largely determined by employers, there is little I can do other than accept what is offered.*

REALITY: Most employers work with *salary ranges* rather than specific figures for positions. Although they may be constrained by rigid pay systems and budgets, they do have some flexibility in deter-

9

mining how much money they will offer for a particular position. The low end of the range will be for individuals who meet the minimum requirements. The upper end of the range will be for attracting individuals with better than average experience. In some organizations the range for a position may be very wide, reflecting a difference of $10-$20,000. For other organizations the range may be only a few hundred or a thousand dollars. The initial offer you receive may be at the bottom of the employer's range. Your goal should be to identify this salary range and put yourself at the top of the range by convincing the employer that you are worth being paid top dollar. How you write your resume, conduct a job interview, and negotiate a compensation package will largely determine where you will fall on the employer's salary range.

MYTH 2:   *Everything is negotiable. If I learn how to effectively negotiate, I should be able to get a much better salary than initially offered by employers.*

REALITY: Some things are negotiable, including many salaries. But for a salary to be negotiable, you must first have a willing partner. If the other party doesn't negotiate, then you have no one to play this game. And some people simply don't negotiate or negotiate very little at all. Indeed, many employers have rigid pay systems that do not allow much flexibility on base pay; they may have more flexibility with benefits. Unfortunately, much of what is written about salary negotiations is most appropriate for large profit-making corporations with 20,000 or more employees and for employees who make over $70,000 a year. Since very few people ever work for such organizations or make that much money, much of the advice is inappropriate for most people (85 percent) who work for small organizations (less than 100 employees) that have less negotiating flexibility on salaries. In fact, many salaries are non-negotiable. The most negotiable salaries are for high-level positions in large corporations requiring a great deal of experience. Even in these organizations, most entry-level positions come with set salaries that are either non-negotiable or involve little salary flexibility. Therefore, if you are first entering the job market or moving to an entry-level position, don't expect to find many employers willing to negotiate your salary. They assign a salary amount to a position which is normally the going market rate. Many small organizations have little flexibility on salaries even in the middle to upper ranks. The same is true for government positions which are assigned ranges on a progressive salary scale. Salaries are pre-set for these positions. The only way to significantly increase your salary in this case is to negotiate the level, grade, or step of the position. You do this by demonstrating that your experience qualifies you to enter at a higher grade level. Compensation for most sales positions involving commissions are determined by one's job performance rather than by negotiating a salary.

MYTH 3:   *I should primarily concentrate on whether or not I will enjoy the job rather than be concerned about how much I will be paid.*

REALITY: You should have no problem finding numerous jobs you will really enjoy. However, many of these jobs pay poorly. Money is important not only for your lifestyle but also as an indicator of your worth. You will do both yourself and your employer a favor if you demonstrate your value and then require the employer to adequately compensate you for your talent. If you fail to address the salary question forthrightly, you may not be respected by the employer who manages to hire you for much less than you are worth. Individuals who can demonstrate their value to employers by translating it into a respectable salary are more likely to do well on the job, because they emphasize what is most important to employers -- job performance. Make sure you get paid for performance rather than the *"going rate"* or a cost-of-living adjustment.

Employers normally try to pay the "going rate" for jobs.

MYTH 4: *The salary I will be offered will reflect what I am worth.*

REALITY: The salary you will be offered will most likely reflect a number of factors, few of which have anything to do with your skills, abilities, and potential performance. Employers normally try to pay the *"going rate"* for jobs. Some may even try to pay as little as possible, depending on how individuals respond to their offers. Employers determine the going rates for salaries by surveying salaries offered for comparable jobs in similar organizations. Your task should be to clearly communicate to employers that they should factor in your value when making salary decisions. Hopefully, you will convince them that your value is well above the going rate.

MYTH 5:   *I'll have a better chance of getting the job if I don't ask too much.*

REALITY: This is the *"penny wise pound foolish"* mentality of extreme bargain shoppers who transfer the same mentality into the job market. While some employers might find hiring the cheapest candidate attractive, most do not since they are shopping for quality employees. And quality is not cheap. Most seasoned employers believe the old adage that *"you get what you pay for"* when hiring people. Their experience confirms this belief. They may pay little for inexperienced people in entry-level positions, but they do so because they don't know what they are getting until the person establishes a track record of performance. Most employers look for *value*, and they give respect to those who price themselves accordingly. If you are too easy and cheap, employers will not see value in you. You will not receive the initial respect you need to get started on the right foot with the employer. Ironically, within certain limits, the higher your price tag, the more value you communicate to employers.

MYTH 6:   *Once I prove myself on the job, I'll be in a better position to negotiate a higher salary.*

REALITY: Unless you somehow become very indispensable to the organization -- the employer simply can't function without you -- and threaten to quit, the initial salary you get may determine what you receive in the long-run, regardless of how well you perform on the job. Once you accept a salary offer, you may have little or no leverage in future salary negotiations. Beware of self-delusions and ego trips to nowhere. Most people think they are worth a lot more to others than they really are. While many feel they are indispensable to the organization, in the eyes of most employers, everyone can be replaced; and many experienced employees are replaceable at lower salaries. When push comes to shove in salary negotiations, many employees who threaten to quit unless their salary demands are met are politely shown the door.

Once you accept a salary offer, you may have little or no leverage in future salary negotiations.

MYTH 7:   *My annual salary increase will reflect my job performance. Therefore, it's important that I work hard and do well on the annual performance appraisal.*

REALITY: Unless you have a written agreement that states future salary increases will be based on perfor-mance, and you know the exact mechanisms used in measuring performance and how they are linked to pay increases, your annual salary increments are more likely to reflect cost-of-living increases than your work efforts. How hard you work or how well you do on an annual perfor-mance appraisal may only determine whether you are retained or fired. Once you are hired, don't expect employers to carefully calculate your future salaries based upon any performance criteria. Indeed, few annual performance ap-praisals are tied to salary considerations. Even the concept of *"merit pay"* is not widely accepted nor practiced in most organizations. To do so might create more internal political turmoil than it's worth since many employees would feel others had unfair advantages because of their close relationship with their supervisors. Therefore, the best salary strategy for most employers is to give all employees across-the-board salary increases reflecting a combination of cost-of-living increases, bonuses, and profit sharing. Employers are better off providing other forms of recognition – especially psychological strokes -- to those who score high on the annual performance appraisal, such as a letter of appreciation, plaque, or an award for being the *"best employee of the month"*.

MYTH 8:   *I should never discuss the issue of salary during an interview.*

REALITY: While it is always best to keep the discussion of salary to the very end – after you know more about the job and you've established your value with the employer -- this is not always possible. Some employers will raise this question early on in order to screen you in or out of their salary range. When this happens, be prepared to discuss salary within the context of *ranges* appropriate for the type of position you are interviewing for. Do not state a specific salary figure you expect since such a figure should be the very last item you agree upon as part of your job offer. At this stage, let the employer know that salary is important to you; that you have done your research on salary comparables; that you expect to receive a salary appropriate for your level of qualifications and experience; and that you want to be compensated on the basis of performance rather than on your past salary history or because of need or greed. What you want to do at this point is get a better idea of what qualifications, experience, and performance are required for this job so you and the employer will have a better idea of what both you and the job are worth. Discuss the salary question at any time, but don't finalize the discussion until you have all the information necessary to determine what will be the best salary for you.

MYTH 9: *When I receive a job offer, I'll have a job.*

REALITY: You only have a job when you've agreed to a specific salary figure and compensation package. In other words, you don't have a job until the employer agrees to give you money in exchange for your talent.

You want to be honest, but there is no need to be stupid.

MYTH 10: *If asked to state my "salary requirements" on an application form or in a cover letter or resume, I should be honest and tell them what I want.*

REALITY: You want to be honest, but there is no need to be stupid at the same time! By stating a salary figure, you may prematurely eliminate yourself from consideration because your salary expectations are either too high or too low! The best response to this question at this stage is that your salary requirements are either *"open"* or *"negotiable"*. If pressed for a specific salary figure, give a range that should be appropriate for the position. You should have such information based upon your research of comparable salaries.

MYTH 11: *Job benefits are often more important than the gross salary figure offered.*

REALITY: While many employers mix salaries with benefits in their discussion of a *"compensation package"*, it's to your advantage to separate salary from benefits and negotiate each starting with your salary. Indeed, some employers may emphasize their excellent benefits, but many do so in order to make their low salary offer look more appealing. Most jobs come with the same or similar package of benefits. Examine the benefits carefully, but settle on a salary figure first. After reaching a salary agreement, turn your attention to the benefits. Consider benefits as something that are expected to come with the job rather than as a part of the salary consideration. If the benefits offered do not meet your minimum standard of what should come with the job, be sure to cost out the missing benefits and include these figures in your salary calculations.

Examine the benefits carefully, but settle on a salary figure first.

MYTH 12: *If I am willing to accept a low starting salary, chances are I can increase my salary substantially within the first year by demonstrating my value to the employer.*

REALITY: The most important salary you will negotiate is your starting salary. Whatever you accept at this point is likely to live with you for a long time. Most employers are not interested in renegotiating a salary you have already accepted. The only way you can substantially increase you salary on-the-job is to move into another job that pays more. This means convincing the employer that you should be promoted to another position that pays more. You do this by demonstrating that you will do well in a higher level position.

MYTH 13: *The longer I work for a company, the more I will be rewarded financially.*

REALITY: The longer you work for a company, the higher the probability your salary will fall behind the salaries of more recently hired personnel who enter the organization at a higher salary level. Your best salary is likely to be your starting salary. After that you will most likely receive yearly salary increments figured as a percentage of your base. Therefore, your starting base salary will be a major determiner of future salary increments. The longer you stay with a company, the more likely you will fall behind others who have been hired more recently. The only ways to substantially increase your salary are to be promoted to a higher level position or leave the company and negotiate a new salary with another employer.

MYTH 14: *I should let my supervisor initiate actions relating to raises and promotions.*

REALITY: While it is always preferable to have your supervisor take such actions, you must also seek visibility beyond your immediate supervisor as well as amongst your co-workers. Let others know -- especially your supervisor's boss -- that you are a producer. Remember, supervisors do change, and personal conflicts with some can stall your career. A co-worker today could well become your supervisor tomorrow. Therefore, it's best to cultivate positive relationships at all levels within your network.

MYTH 15: *Money will not make you happy.*

REALITY: Neither will poverty. This is a good rationalization for not doing as well financially as one could and should. And you will be especially unhappy when you learn you are getting paid less than you're worth or less than others in the organization with comparable experience and skills. There's a lot of truth to the saying that *"Those who think money can't bring happiness don't know where to shop!"* You'll be especially happy when you get a salary commensurate with your value. While money may not make you happy, it makes life much more *convenient*. Better yet, it helps you *keep score* on your level of success in the world of work. The higher your salary, the more value you are to the employer. Don't undersell yourself because of some beliefs about the role of money in life. It's okay for talented people to make lots of money.

MAJOR SALARY MISTAKES

If myths were not enough to prevent many people from dealing with the salary question, numerous mistakes also are made by many people concerning salary. The major such mistakes are that they:

- Avoid facing the salary question head-on in terms of goals, salary ranges, and negotiating techniques.

- Fail to do research on salary comparables and thus are unprepared to deal with salary questions and issues with employers.

- Don't know how much they are worth.

- Reveal a specific salary figure when asked about their *"salary requirements"*.

- Assume their *"qualifications"* and *"performance"* will determine their salary level.

- Think salaries are predetermined by employers.

- Believe they are indispensable to employers who will give them substantial raises rather than risk loosing them to the competition.

- Under-value their worth.

- Over-value their worth.

- Think employers are always in the driver's seat when it comes to negotiating salary and terms of employment.

- Approach salary negotiations from a perspective of need or greed rather than as a process of assigning value to their qualifications and promises of performance.

- Prematurely discuss salary before acquiring information on the job as well as communicating their qualifications to employers.

- Fail to compile *supports* for a negotiating position.

- Don't know how to close and follow-up the salary negotiation interview.

- Forget to calculate benefits as part of the compensation package.

- Put too much emphasis on benefits rather than concentrate on the gross salary figure.

- Project an image that is not commensurate with the salary being negotiated.

- Put too high a price tag on themselves without providing supports to justify the salary figure.

- Negotiate salary and benefits over the telephone.

- Are too quick to accept employers' first or second offers.

- Don't know how to use *timing* as part of establishing their value in the eyes of employers.

- Fail to adequately assess the employer's needs and develop a strategy to meet those needs as well as relate this strategy to their salary requirements.

- Fail to raise intelligent salary questions of employers.

- Don't know how to handle employer's salary questions or say the wrong things.

- Don't give themselves much room to negotiate.

- Don't know when to leave a job or company for opportunities elsewhere that will pay better.

MONEY IN YOUR FUTURE

The following pages are designed to dispel these myths as well as help you avoid the many mistakes made by others when dealing with compensation questions. Our overall emphasis is on how you can best communicate your qualifications to employers as you eventually translate your value into an acceptable salary for both you and the employer. If you can do this, you should be well on the road to achieving higher salaries in the years to come. While this money may not bring you happiness, at least it will add greater value to your qualifications as well as help you better keep score on your progress in the job market as you continue to advance your career!

Chapter Three

FUTURE SALARY AND BENEFIT TRENDS

Salary is only one, albeit the most important, component of employee compensation. While many employers separate salary from benefits, other employers view the two together as a *"compensation package"*. For them, a salary may only comprise 65 percent of what may be an attractive package of employer-sponsored health, life, and disability insurance; paid vacations and leave; education and training opportunities; child care services; generous stock options and profit sharing; and an early retirement plan. For other employers, salary may comprise 90 percent of total compensation. For many job seekers and employees, the compensation package appears confusing and somewhat mystical.

KNOW THE VALUE OF JOBS

When dealing with the question of salary, be sure you know what the total compensation package looks like as well as how much it is worth in dollar terms. While most benefits come with the job and thus are not negotiable, some may be negotiable, especially in situations where employers offer flexible benefit options. Moreover, the benefits offered by one employer may add up to a substantial financial advantage over the compensation packages of other employers.

Information on the total salary and benefit package is important for comparing compensation among employers and for determining how much a *position* is really worth in comparison to other positions. A $30,000 salary with one employer, for example, may be part of a $42,000 compensation package, whereas this same salary makes up most of a $35,000 compensation package with another employer. For during the last three decades the trend has been toward increasing employee benefits at a higher rate than salaries. In general, base wages remain the most inflexible element in compensation packages. Large and progressive companies have led the way in expanding employee benefits. However, this trend is likely to be reversed in the coming decade as base wages receive greater attention in employee compensation packages.

During the last three decades the trend has been toward increasing employee benefits at a higher rate than salaries.

TOWARD GREATER BENEFITS AND SECURITY

Much of the history of worker compensation is a 20th century story of how government and employers took greater responsibility in ensuring the income, health, and old age security of workers in the form of benefits financed through payroll taxes, retirement funds, and shared employer-employee benefit programs. Prior to the 1930s, most workers primarily worked for wages. Insurance and retirement plans were largely the responsibilities of workers who, at best, would save for their own retirement as well as find private forms of health, disability, and life insurance.

All this changed in the 1930s with the advent of government-sponsored social security and the increasing role of private insurance companies and pension organizations in providing protection against the income, health, and old age insecurities of the work place and life in general. Such legislation as the Social Security Act and the Wagner Act of 1935 put in motion new wage and benefit initiatives, financed largely through payroll taxes, that would continue to the present day. Protection against income insecurities was primarily seen as a government and employer responsibility. Employees participated indirectly through shared systems of financing. By moving the primary financing responsibilities to government and employers, the costs of such programs were cut dramatically as workers participated in group benefit plans.

The initial emphasis on income protection against the twin problems of old age and unemployment expanded to cover a variety of other worker benefits during the post World War II period: paid holidays and vacations, insurance, pensions, wages, hours, working conditions, bonuses, stock options, and saving plans. Indeed, the general trend during the past 40 years has been to increase worker benefits at a much faster rate than wages. Consequently, benefits make up a larger share of compensation packages today than 40 years ago. Most compensation packages also reflect the structure of a pre-1970s society in which a male head of household was the sole wage earner providing for a non-wage earning spouse and children. Insurance plans, for example, providing coverage for all members of the family are central benefits for many workers.

Much of the credit for developing the benefits side of employee compensation packages must be given to the role of unions and the collective bargaining process. At the height of their membership in 1945, when over 35 percent of the work force was unionized, and throughout the 1950s, unions pressed for greater benefits along with higher wages. However, union membership began to steadily decline starting in the 1960s to where only about 16 percent of today's work force belongs to unions. As the economy in the early 1980s went through a major recession, with unemployment hitting 11 percent, and with numerous plant closures in declining industries, unions shifted their emphasis toward greater job security for workers threatened with layoffs and permanent displacement.

Indeed, salary *"give backs"* and benefit reductions became new elements in the collective bargaining process as unions reluctantly accepted wage and benefit decreases for assurances of long-term job security.

At the same time, new initiatives centering around retirement programs, such as lump sum payments to encourage early retirement, and flexible benefits, were instituted in many companies, including government. As a health care financing crisis loomed in the future for most health care programs, cost containment became a major issue for employers who were paying escalating health insurance premiums. Consequently, more and more health benefit programs shifted from 100 percent employer financing to shared funding by employer and employee. Some two-tiered benefit programs were also instituted wherein newly hired employees received fewer benefits than those already working in the organization. However, these initiatives have not become widespread and many will most likely disappear in the near future.

Cost containment became a major issue for employers who were paying escalating health insurance premiums.

While wages during the 1980s did increase, the changes were incremental, largely reflecting cost-of-living increases due to inflation. Benefits began to be restructured in response to the changing nature of the American work force -- the advent of working spouses who received similar and often overlapping benefit packages – and the high cost of health care.

25 FUTURE TRENDS

The 1980s was a major watershed period for the evolution of wage and benefit policies. Several structural changes in the economy and population placed into motion new trends for compensation packages in the 1980s and beyond. The major impetus for these changes during the early 1980s were poor economic conditions coupled with an ailing economy in need of major restructuring in the face of a highly competitive international economic environment. Other significant developments impacting on compensation included the changing structure of the American family; declining union power; dying industries; the deregulation of transportation and communication industries; skyrocketing cost of medical care; and a bulging national deficit. These changes would most likely continue throughout the 1990s as well as into the first part of the 21st century.

The most important trends for salary and benefits appear to be in the following directions for the coming decade:

1. *More flexibility in compensation packages:* Given the evolution of the two-career family where spouses have similar benefit coverage, more and more employers will offer flexible compensation packages and reimbursement accounts that provide options for their employees. The key concept here is *options*. Compensation packages will be structured so they can be custom-designed around the needs of different types of employees. For example, more and more companies will offer their employees a menu of benefits from which to choose: life, health, and long-term disability insurance as well as cash, personal leave, and child care services. An employee who already receives health insurance coverage on his or her spouse's policy might elect to take a cash option rather than receive duplicate health insurance coverage.

2. *Salary increases will be more closely tied to cost-of-living increases:* Regardless of all the talk about performance appraisals, merit pay, and rewarding individual productivity, few employers will actually institute compensation policies tied to such performance criteria. Cost-of-living increases will continue to be the major determinant of salary increases for current employees in most organizations. Performance will most

likely continue to be rewarded with bonuses, promotions, and other forms of employer recognition other than salary increases. The single most important factor determining major salary increases for individuals will be a job promotion within an organization or a job change to another organization. These are the times when salary negotiations play a central role in determining compensation.

3. *"Give backs" will continue in declining industries:* As union power further declines and as unions remain focused on guaranteeing long-term job security, employees will continue to accept employer demands for lower salaries and scaled-down benefits in exchange for job security.

4. *Salary caps will continue with government salaries:* Regardless of all the self-serving comparable salary studies emphasizing that compensation of government employees lags behind those in the private sector, legislators will continue to put caps on the highest salaries paid in government at the Federal, state, and local levels. These caps will further deter *"the best and the brightest"* from pursuing long-term government careers.

5. *Highest paying salaries and attractive benefit packages will go to such high demand occupations as chemical and petroleum engineers:* Salaries generally follow labor market supply and demand trends. Occupations experiencing major labor shortages tend to offer higher salaries. The lowest and least negotiable salaries tend to be for entry-level positions as well as those with an over-supply of job applicants.

6. *Few employees have bargaining power to substantially increase their base salaries and benefits in most organizations:* Once hired, most individuals have little say in determining their salary increases. Employers attempt to be both equitable and secret in determining

salary increases. The equitable strategy results in treating all employees the same on the question of salary -- give them cost of living increases as a percentage of their base salary. This equitable strategy is also an administratively expedient one that best conforms to the rigid pay systems found in many organizations.

7. *Compensation packages will increasingly reflect the changing nature of the work force and society:* Greater emphasis will be placed on flextime, day-care services, parental leave, unpaid leave, benefit options, and employee contributions to the escalating cost of health insurance.

8. *More emphasis will be placed on salary increases as the benefit share of compensation declines:* While the 1980s was a period for expanding benefits, the 1990s will see more attention focused on salaries and increasing the portability of retirement benefits. Therefore, negotiating salaries will be more important than examining benefit packages which will be largely predetermined and similar for most organizations.

9. *Salary negotiations will be most successful for high level professional and technical positions:* Most blue collar and lower level professional and technical positions, many of which are entry-level, involve fixed salaries that are only negotiable within very narrow ranges. High demand positions, as well as high level positions that are most important to organizations, will have the greatest salary flexibility.

10. *Salaries and salary ranges will be most difficult to identify for professional and technical positions:* The salaries for most blue collar and lower level professional and technical positions are relatively easy to identify given the public nature of these salaries. State and local government agencies regularly gather salary data on these positions, and many classified ads state

the salary ranges for such positions. However, publicized data on higher-level professional and technical positions are not so readily available. Consequently, you must conduct your own research in order to identify the salary ranges for such positions.

11. *Retirement plans will increasingly emphasize portability and early-out options in both the public and private sectors:* The old *"golden handcuff"* pension systems of limited portability will give way to greater portability so that employees can more readily change jobs and careers. Defined contribution plans, largely replacing the traditional defined benefit retirement plans, will enable employees to more easily transfer accumulated retirement benefits with one employer to another. Declining industries, including government, will increasingly offer employees early-out retirement options in order to reduce their on-going payroll obligations.

12. *Life, health, and disability insurance payments will increasingly be shared by both employers and employees:* The health care insurance crisis in particular will lead the way for restructuring traditional insurance benefits. More and more insurance programs will require greater financial contributions on the part of employees.

13. *Unions will continue to play a minor role in the structure of compensation packages:* The decline of unions, which began in earnest during the 1970s, is likely to accelerate as the traditional union bases -- agriculture and manufacturing -- continue to decline.

14. *Collective bargaining will increasingly be dominated by employers who largely determine the structure of compensation packages.* As unions continue to decline and new employee-employer collective bargaining mechanisms evolve, expect employers to play the dominant role in the collective bargaining process.

15. *Except for high demand occupations, employers will be increasingly reluctant to negotiate salaries and benefits in the highly volatile economy of the 1990s:* Salaries will be largely pre-determined, within narrow ranges, for most positions. As in the 1980s, employers will not be anxious to pay more than the norm unless they experience serious difficulty in recruiting new personnel.

16. *Initial starting salaries will continue to be the major determinant of future salary increases for most employees:* Your starting salary will be your most important salary today and tomorrow. Most employers will continue to figure salary increases as a percentage of employee's base salary. Therefore, it's imperative that you start at the highest salary possible, because this will be the last highest salary you will ever receive within the organization. Unless you become indispensable to the organization or receive a major promotion, the next time you will receive a significant salary increase is when you quit your job and get hired by another organization that is willing to pay you a substantially higher salary.

17. *The coming labor shortages of the 1990s will not have a significant impact on the structure of salaries and benefits:* Most of the labor shortage is concentrated at the lowest level of the labor force – unskilled hourly workers who receive minimum wage. While some wage inflation will take place at this level due to supply and demand problems, increases in salaries and benefits at this level will be insignificant compared to other segments in the labor force.

18. *Child care benefits and parental leave will become more important elements in compensation packages:* Family care benefits will increasingly play an important role for two-career couples who are concerned that their jobs and careers not be detrimental to their family situations. The demand for liberal parental leave for

both men and women rather than the traditional maternal leave for women will become part of compensation packages along with innovative child care benefits. Unpaid leave will become an important issue for employees with dependent care responsibilities – the birth of a child or illness of a child, spouse, or parent.

19. *Reimbursement accounts will offer employees new options for reducing their taxes as well as increasing the extent of employer financed benefit coverage:* More and more employees will negotiate reduced salaries for the tax advantages of reimbursement accounts that will pay their share of insurance premiums, health care deductibles, and child care.

20. *Cost containment for medical insurance will continue to be a major issue in the decade ahead and will be reflected in differential compensation packages:* The cost of medical care will continue to outpace increases in the general cost of living. Given the high costs of medical care, health and disability insurance benefits will be the most highly sought after employee benefits. Many employees will be less concerned with their overall salary figure than with the percentage coverage of and the employer contribution to the health insurance package. Employers, in turn, will continue to push for restructuring health benefits so they include a larger employee contribution to the cost of premiums. Compensation differentials between employers who provide 100 percent medical coverage with no deductibles and those who only provide partial coverage with some deductibles may be great, depending on the family health needs of individual employees.

21. *Supplemental pay will continue to play an important role in compensation systems:* Basic salary will remain the most rigid form of compensation. Once a pay system is in place, including upward adjustment policies, few employers have any interest in altering it

in response to individual circumstances. Instead, employers have greater flexibility in offering lump-sum payments, nonproduction bonuses, profit sharing plans, reimbursement accounts, and overtime in addition to the base pay rates. These supplemental pay options will continue to expand in the decade ahead in response to the compensation needs of different employees.

22. *More comprehensive and flexible paid leave policies will be offered by employers:* More and more companies will adopt flexible annual leave policies that give employees opportunities to accumulate and defer paid leave for different leave situations -- personal, sick, vacation, military, funeral, holiday.

23. *More innovative and attractive compensation packages will be developed as recruitment strategies in a highly competitive labor market:* The coming decade will witness major labor shortages due to a slow growing labor force with fewer young people entering the work force. In efforts to recruit from this dwindling pool of traditional entry-level employees, more and more employers will emphasize attractive compensation packages, complete with bonuses, savings plans, child care, educational benefits, and health coverage.

24. *More and more contingency workers will enter the job market primarily for the purpose of acquiring attractive benefits rather than for receiving significant salaries:* A growing army of temporary workers that are leased or contracted-out to clients will continue to expand. Since limited but attractive benefits are offered by firms managing such workers, more people will be attracted to such working arrangements which also give them the advantage of a more flexible work life.

25. *Small businesses will compete more favorably with large businesses on compensation packages:* More and more small businesses will contract-out their compensation packages to firms specializing in group benefit

programs. These arrangements will make small business more competitive on the benefit side of compensation.

FLEXIBILITY IN YOUR FUTURE

These salary and benefit trends raise several important issues you need to consider when addressing the compensation question with potential employers or with your present employer. No longer is compensation a simple issue of how much salary and how many paid vacation days you will receive. Compensation today deals with complex social issues that reflect the changing structure of American society and the work force. These issues affect most workers, be it medical insurance, child care, unpaid leave for dependent care, paid leave, education and training reimbursements, portable retirement systems, early retirement, or reimbursement accounts. These benefits can add up to a sizeable proportion of one's compensation. Indeed, you may discover that nearly 30 percent of compensation with some employers comes in the form of benefits.

The key dynamic in compensation packages today is *flexibility*. More options and more choices will continue to be offered in the decade ahead as employers adjust to a restructured society and work force of the 1990s.

At the same time, don't expect to negotiate many benefits with employers. While some employers will have flexible benefit packages that enable you to select from a menu of choices, most benefits come with the job. What you most need to know is your *options* and how these options add up in terms of total compensation. With this information, you can compare one employer to another and decide whether the $30,000 job offer with Employer X is equivalent to the $30,000 job offer with Employer Y. Indeed, you may discover that Employer X's $30,000 is actually $35,000 whereas Employer Y's $30,000 means $42,000 in total compensation.

These compensation differentials are also important for your future earnings power. For example, when employers ask you for your salary history, you need not state $30,000 since your total compensation package translates into a much higher dollar figure. Instead, talk in terms of the cash equivalent of the package. Therefore, a $30,000 salary is actually $42,000 in compensation with Employer Y. Needless to say, working for Employer Y will have a much more positive impact on your total earnings than working for Employer X. We'll return to this strategic negotiation point when we examine different salary negotiation strategies in Chapter Eight.

Chapter Four

KNOW WHAT
YOU'RE WORTH

What exactly are you worth to an employer? Do you have intrinsic value due to past achievements, or is your value largely determined by the going market rate for someone with your skills or for the position or job you wish to acquire? Or perhaps you're only worth what others in similar positions within the organization are being paid?

Knowing what you are worth is one of the most important yet difficult questions to answer. However, if you don't know your value before applying for a position, you may well apply for the wrong job as well as under-value or over-value yourself in the eyes of employers.

POSITIONS VERSUS INDIVIDUALS

Let's start by making a distinction between positions and individuals and then examine the calculations involved in assigning salaries to positions but awarding them to individuals. Employers hire individuals to fill positions within their organization. They first value the position and then attempt to find individuals with sufficient skills to perform well in the position.

On the other hand, individuals seek positions that offer them maximum value. They are more concerned- with their own value than with the value of the position. While both the employer and employee focus their attention on the position, their concepts of what is being valued may differ considerably.

How, then, do employers value positions and their employees? Within every organization you will find a hierarchy of salaries which are assigned to positions. The range between the lowest and highest salaries may be great. Indeed, the lowest paid workers may be hourly custodial and clerical personnel who work for near minimum wage. The top salary may be $150,000 or more, depending on the organization. Expect to see at least a 1 to 25 ratio between the lowest and highest salaries in most organizations with 100 or more employees.

Salary ranges do not differ greatly from one organization to another, although they may appear so to many people who think a few thousand dollars makes a big difference. In general, most entry-level positions will be valued under $20,000 a year, although some hard-to-fill entry-level positions may pay $30,000 or more. Technical and middle management positions will be in the $30,000 to $40,000 range, depending on the level of responsibility. Overall, 80 percent of the employees in most organizations will be making under $30,000 a year.

CALCULATING THE *"GOING RATE"*

While some employers may try to hire personnel at the cheapest rate possible, most employers are more realistic and thus price positions according to the *"going rate"*. The going rate is largely determined by internal and external salary comparisons as well as current market considerations:

- The internal salary structure of the organization.

- Salaries for similar positions found in other organizations within the industry as well as the region.

• What the market will bear at any particular time given current labor supply and demand considerations.

When it comes to salaries, most employers do not want to be pace-setters by offering the highest salaries, nor do they want to be known for being *"cheap"* by paying the lowest salaries. Most are satisfied with just being *"average"* or a little above the norm. In general, however, the largest and most successful companies tend to pay the best and thus serve as pacesetters for employers in other companies. Few companies ever become successful because they pay cheap wages.

The most successful companies tend to pay the best and thus serve as pacesetters for employers in other companies.

At the same time, most employers prefer making salaries equitable, secret, non-negotiable, and easily administered. They try to keep salaries *equitable* within the organization by not paying anyone much above the internal norm. To do otherwise would appear unfair should others within the organization learn about salary differentials and begin comparing their salaries with those of others who may or may not be as productive. After all, individuals who manage to negotiate higher salaries tend to be those who take initiative concerning their salaries. They get higher salaries because of their negotiating skills and political savvy rather than their increased productivity.

Secrecy is necessary to best deal with the salary inequities that inherently arise due to the nature of the hiring and promotion processes. Without secrecy, considerable internal dissension might ensue should long-term employees discover that a new employee managed to get hired at a much higher salary than employees already working for -- and more loyal to -- the organization.

Ideally, then, employers prefer keeping salaries *non-negotiable,* because to negotiate with individuals inevitably means creating individual salary inequities as well as uncomfortable employee-employer situations that are best avoided if possible.

The best way to deal with the salary issue is put into place a pay system that can be *easily administered* to everyone, a system where no special individual compensation agreements exist. Such a system would appear to be fair to all. Indeed, should salaries become publicized, a pay system would help minimize the amount of internal conflict because salaries will appear to be equitably assigned and distributed.

---

*Most employers prefer keeping
salaries both equitable
and secret.*

Overall, the tendency toward paying the *"norm"* is strong among most employers. They regularly seek comparative salary information to make sure they are playing the salary game within existing norms. Thinking around the norm is manifested in questions employers ask about salaries. For example, should you ask for a salary higher than the norm, the first two questions employers will raise as objections, and which you must respond to, are:

- *But that's much more than others are paid in this industry as well as in our area. Why should we pay more?*

- *How can we justify paying you that much when others in our organization with comparable skills and experience are making less?*

Going beyond your general desire to get a higher salary because you want it, need it, and feel you deserve it, how will you respond to these questions with facts about your value that support your request? Your problem, then, is to help the employer break out of this norm thinking that is centered around positions rather than focused on you as a unique and exceptional individual who promises to perform above the norm. Therefore, you want to focus on the employer's problems and bottom line rather than on your need or greed. Your approaches and salary strategies should be employer-centered rather than self-centered.

> *You want to focus on the employer's problems and bottom line rather than on your need or greed.*

If the employer wants to attract top talent, then he or she expects to pay above the going rate and beyond the internal norm for the organization. If you want to justify a higher than expected salary, you'll have to convince the employer that you are above the norm in terms of your potential performance. On the other hand, for most entry-level positions, salaries offered will be very close to the norm for the companies in the industry and in the same geographic area. Expect little negotiation to take place for such positions unless you show exceptional promise for someone with little or no experience.

While employers know how to price positions, they also have ways of valuing *individuals*. The easiest way of determining what you are worth is to learn what you were paid in your last job. If, for example, last year you made $25,000, in the eyes of most employers you are probably worth no more than an additional 10 to 15 percent − maybe $30,000 a year. If you ask for $50,000 and the employer knows you made only $25,000, he or she may feel you are overvaluing yourself. Depending on what percentage increase you expect over your last salary, it may also be to your advantage to keep your salary history secret!

Most employers know what the going rate is for positions, because they keep in contact with several sources of comparative salary information. The most widely used sources include:

- *Professionals in other organizations who may trade salary information on comparable positions.* They may occasionally ask each other *"By the way, what is your organization paying these days for X, Y, and Z positions? What about benefits?"*

- *Salary surveys of professional associations, executive search firms, and local employment agencies.* If, for example, they are interviewing graduating college seniors for entry-level positions, they may consult the latest quarterly report of the College Placement Council's *CPC Salary Survey.*

- *Classified ads in newspapers, magazines, and trade journals which list salaries offered for particular positions and organizations.* Many of these ads will state a specific salary figure or a salary range, depending on the experience of the applicant.

- *Job applicants who state salary requirements.* By interviewing applicants and asking them about their salary requirements, employers get first-hand salary information on their immediate market -- those they are likely to hire.

Employers also know their internal salary structure as well as yearly cost-of-living increases. What they don't know initially is your past salary history as well as your salary demands. They need this information in order to determine your value in reference to the value of the position so they can make you what they consider to be both a *"reasonable"* and *"appropriate"* salary offer.

Consequently, based on the salary calculations of employers, you are potentially worth the *"going rate"* plus or minus your present salary and your potential to add value to the organization. Put another way, before you even state your salary requirements, the employer is likely to offer you a salary that reflects two basic elements in his or her salary calculations:

• The value of the position as determined by the employer's various information sources on comparables within and outside the organization.

• Your value as determined by your salary history.

If, for example, you are interviewing for a position valued at $40,000 a year, but your most recent salary was $20,000 a year, you may have difficulty even receiving a job offer at the $40,000 level, regardless of how impressive you are on paper as well as in the interview. You simply don't have the salary track record to justify $40,000 a year or more. This employer logic for determining your value is inherently at odds with your own logic that places emphasis on your inherent worth as judged by your performance rather than by others' pay or your salary history.

You must convince the employer that you are a capable individual who will bring additional value to the organization that is above the norm.

How, then, do you determine your value and translate it into a salary figure so that you can best communicate your value to employers who, in turn, must translate it into a specific salary offer? We suggest you follow the same logic as the employer, but add one new element – your *capabilities* as translated into the employer's language of organizational performance. Prior to performing on the job you must convince the employer that you are a capable individual who will bring additional value to the organization that is above the norm for this and other organizations. In other words, you are an exceptional individual whose talents are worth much more than the average employee. You must be specific here. Can you, for example, demonstrate beyond lofty promises that your work is likely to generate an additional $250,000 in profits for the organization? By concentrating on your capabilities and potential performance, you *raise* the employer's expectations and thereby create an additional element of value in the salary calculation that goes beyond salary comparables and a salary figure assigned to a position. In so doing, you transcend the position by focusing the salary question on you as an *individual*.

Above all, you need to do research on salaries prior to interviewing for a job. Your research will involve examining salary studies and talking to people with salary information.

DETERMINE SALARY COMPARABLES

With a few exceptions, both you and the employer have access to the same sources of information on salary comparables. The major exception is information on the salary rates within the employer's organization. Such information is usually a closely held secret that only a few well placed individuals in the organization share with each other in the process of making salary decisions. Since you most likely will not get access to this information, you must guess what this pay system looks like based upon your research of salaries offered by comparable organizations.

Salary Studies and Surveys

Numerous salary surveys are conducted by the government, corporations, associations, employment firms, newspapers, and magazines. While some of these studies are public information, others are confidential studies only available to paying clients. Some of the best and most accessible surveys are found in your local library, college placement office, or employment firms.

A good starting point is to consult several books that compile salary information from numerous salary surveys and focus it around discussions of particular occupational fields. We highly recommend acquiring a copy of the latest edition of John Wright's *The American Almanac of Jobs and Salaries* (New York: Avon Books). Published every two to three years, each edition is a compendium of salary information compiled from numerous salary studies conducted by government, associations, and private firms.

Other books, such as the Department of Labor's *Occupational Outlook Handbook*, National Textbook's *Opportunities in...* series, and Career Press' *Career Directory* series, include salary information on hundreds of occupations. These books are widely available in libraries and bookstores. They can also be ordered directly from Impact Publications by completing the order information at the end of this book.

Beyond the books that interpret salary data are the actual salary surveys that present the raw data in statistical tables. The major salary surveys are conducted annually by the following organizations:

- *Department of Labor:*   The Bureau of Labor Statistics monitors salaries for numerous occupations nationwide. Its findings are published in several quarterly reports for regions and the nation as a whole: *Industry Wage Surveys, Area Wage Surveys, White-Collar Pay,* and *Employee Benefits Survey.* Another publication, the *Monthly Labor Review* which is Bureau's monthly journal, regularly summarizes this statistical information. Many libraries have copies of these reports and the journal, or they can be examined in the Bureau of Labor Statistics regional offices which are located in Boston, New York City, Philadelphia, Atlanta, Chicago, Dallas, Kansas City, San Francisco, and Washington, DC.

- *U.S. Office of Personnel Management:*   Compiles salary information on government employees at the Federal, state, and local levels. The Office of Personnel Management library in Washington, DC will have this information.

- *State and local governments:*   Many state and local governments conduct salary and wage surveys for occupations within their geographic area. Contact your state employment commission or county or municipal personnel office to find out if they have such salary information. Your local library should also have information on such surveys. While many of these surveys primarily focus on blue collar occupations within certain industries, some will also include professional and technical positions. While much of this data may be too generalized by industry to be useful in determining salary ranges for particular positions, it will give you some idea of average salaries paid in your particular geographic area.

• *Executive search, employment, and consulting firms:* Many executive search, employment, and consulting firms conduct their own salary surveys of selected occupations. Some firms are commissioned to do these surveys for corporate clients whereas others compile this information for advertising and public relations purposes. For example, Robert Half International, a job placement firm with over 150 offices nationwide as well as in Canada, the United Kingdom, and Isreal, each year publishes the *Robert Half Salary Survey* for positions in accounting, finance, banking, and information systems. Available in booklet form, you can get a free copy of this report by calling any Robert Half office. Other noted firms conducting salary studies include Hewitt Associates, Battelle Memorial Institute, and D. Dietrich Associates. While most of these studies are conducted for clients, some are also sold to the general public. While very expensive to acquire, some of the salary information appearing in these studies will periodically appear in major magazines and newspapers, such as *Working Women* and *The Wall Street Journal.*

• *Trade and professional associations:* One of the best and most reliable sources for salary information by occupation and geographic area are the more than 3,000 trade and professional associations that are primarily headquartered in Washington, DC, New York City, and Chicago. Most of these associations conduct an annual salary survey of their members. Usually published in one issue of their newsletter or magazine, the survey identifies who makes how much and where. The National Association of Broadcasters, for example, publishes an annual compensation and fringe benefit report that outlines the average salaries of its members. The American Association of University Professors also publishes an annual salary survey for higher education. The American Federation of Teachers as well as the National Education Association publish similar surveys for elementary and secondary teachers. If you are interested in salaries for engineers, contact the National Society of Professional Engineers which also conducts its own annual salary survey. If you are interested in surveying entry-level salaries offered by the major college recruiters, you should examine the College Placement Council's quarterly and annual *CPC Salary Survey* which is available in many college and university offices of career planning and placement. If you are not familiar with these associations, the best place to start are two useful directories found in the reference section of most libraries: *The Encyclopedia of Associations* (Detroit, MI: Gale Research) and the *National Trade and Professional Associations* (Washington, DC: Columbia Books). Revised annually, these two directories provide contact information and summaries on more than 20,000 domestic and international associations. If you can't find an association relevant to your particular occupation in these two directories, you can safely assume that no such association exists. Once you locate an appropriate association, call their main office and ask if they have information on salary ranges for your particular occupational specialty.

• *Journals and magazines:* Numerous journals and magazines also conduct salary studies as well as publicize the survey findings of other organizations. *Adweek*, for example, publishes a annual salary survey for the advertising field. *Fortune* and *Inc.* magazines usually reveals the salaries of CEOs in the Fortune 500 companies. The *Public Relations Journal* publishes salaries of public relations professionals. The January issue of *Working Woman* usually pulls together numerous salary surveys of associations, employment firms, government, and magazines in its annual salary survey issue. *Com-*

pensation Review keeps compensation specialists informed on salaries and benefits with their industries.

• *Newspapers:* Some newspapers will occasionally conduct their own salary surveys among industries within their community. Others report the survey findings of various salary studies.

Classified Ads and Job Listings

Two of the most important sources for salary information are the classified sections of newspapers, magazines, trade journals, and newsletters and job listings available through employment offices. Many employment ads will reveal the salaries or salary ranges being offered for particular positions. By periodically surveying these ads, you may get a fairly accurate idea of who is paying what in your geographic area.

Employment offices, both public and private, are repositories for job vacancy announcements and other information on salaries. Employers listing with these offices normally include the salary ranges for each position announced.

However, don't expect to find salaries listed for all types of positions. Salaries for blue-collar and hourly positions will most often appear in classified ads and in employment offices. While some ads and vacancy announcements may list the salaries for higher level professional and technical positions, many do not. Invariably they will include general statements such as *"salary and benefits commensurate with qualifications and experience"* or *"we offer a competitive salary and an excellent fringe benefit package"*. Alternatively, the ad may request that you submit your salary history, salary requirements, or salary expectations along with your resume when applying for the position. These statements and instructions, in effect, notify you that there is flexibility with the salary and thus it is negotiable within certain limits as determined by both the employer and your salary history.

One of the best sources for salary information on professional and technical positions is the *National Business Employment Weekly* of the *Wall Street Journal*. This newspaper includes hundreds of classified ads from all over the country as well as from abroad. Many of the ads will include a specific salary or salary range or notify you they are competitive and that you should submit your salary history. The Sunday editions of major newspapers such as *The New York Times, Washington Post,* and the *Los Angeles Times* will include extensive listings of professional and technical positions. If you survey a few issues of these newspapers, you should be able to get a sense of what employers are offering for the type of position you are seeking -- at least in those specific metropolitan areas.

Be sure to survey your own local newspaper and related publications. While newspapers in major metropolitan areas will provide you with salary information for positions in major cities, many of these advertisements may reflect salaries that are 20 to 30 percent higher than in most other communities. Therefore, the classified ads appearing in your local newspaper should more accurately reflect the pricing of jobs in your community. Survey these major national publications, but also know what is being offered locally.

Special Reports and Projects

You may also discover special reports and projects that include information on salaries. Faculty and research offices at your local college and university may regularly conduct salary surveys and publish their results in reports that have limited distribution beyond their immediate institution. You may also discover special job search projects that include information on salaries. For example, in our own state of Virginia, a computerized job search program called Virginia View includes information on salary ranges both within Virginia and nationwide for numerous types of positions. Centered at Virginia Tech in Blacksburg, Virginia, this program is available throughout the state at most college and university career planning and placement offices as well as in many local libraries and state employment offices. The project also includes a toll-free Career Information Hotline number for state residents in need of job and career assistance: 800/542-5870. You may find similar types of projects operating in your state or local community. Contact your local library, state employment office, or college and university career planning and placement office for information on any such special reports and projects.

Networking for Information

The final source of information for salaries and salary ranges for determining your value will be your own networking activities. Indeed, this may well become the best and most reliable source of information on salaries that most directly relates to the type of position you are seeking.

Networking plays a central role in any well organized and targeted job search. It involves the process of contacting individuals for information, advice, and referrals in reference to your job search. It encompasses a specific set of targeted activities that will eventually yield nonadvertized job opportunities. Your networking might include talking to relatives, neighbors, friends, colleagues, and acquaintances or making new contacts with strangers, including employment specialists and potential employers who have information on the types of jobs you are seeking. While you will want to gather a great deal of word-of-mouth information from these people on job vacancies, qualifications, responsibilities, work environments, and advancement opportunities, you also want to ask questions about salaries and compensation packages. For example, as part of your informational interviewing activities, you should pose one of two simple nonthreatening salary research questions:

What is the normal salary range for this type of job?

or

What do individuals with these qualifications and levels of responsibility normally make in this industry? And what are the fringe benefits that normally come with this job?

As we will see later, these are the same types of questions you may want to ask an interviewer if he or she raises the issue of salary early on in the interview. This question will quickly yield salary information from individuals who know exactly what is being paid for the type of job that most interests you. When conducting informational interviews as part of your networking activities, under no circumstances should you ask the person you are interviewing about their salary. People are much more willing to reveal salary information on others than on themselves. They consider such a directed question an invasion of their privacy. Therefore, make sure you direct the salary question away from the individual as you attempt to determine the value of jobs and positions rather than the person you are interviewing.

The networking process and the methodology for conducting the informational interview are outlined in detail in two of our other books: *Network Your Way to Job and Career Success* and *Interview for Success*.

People are much more willing to reveal salary information on others than on themselves.

CONDUCT YOUR OWN SALARY SURVEY

The most productive way to determine the value of positions, as well as your own value, is to conduct your own salary survey. This involves a five-step procedure for gathering salary information on the positions and organizations that most interest you.

1. *Read literature on jobs and salary ranges.* Recommended readings include *The American Almanac of Jobs and Salaries* and *The Occupational Outlook Handbook,* and numerous salary reports issued by the U.S. Department of Labor's Bureau of Labor Statistics. Many of these salary reports are summarized in the Bureau of Labor Statistics' journal, the *Monthly Labor Review.* All of these resources should be available in your local library.

2. *Visit your local library for information.* Local libraries and librarians are precious resources for conducting a job search as well as for gathering comparative salary

information. If you are not an expert on library resources, it's best to approach the information desk or someone in the reference section and ask them about resources on salary ranges. Experienced librarians are wonderful sources for all types of information. Tell them exactly what you are doing and let them solve your problem by directing you to their resources. For example, approach them in the following manner:

> *I'm in the process of gathering information on salaries for jobs in _____. What might be some good information sources you could recommend? For example, do you have the salary survey reports of the Bureau of Labor Statistics or similar surveys conducted by state and local government agencies? Do you know of anyone who might have this information?*

You may be surprised by the wealth of information and cooperation this question generates! In addition to directing you to the appropriate in-house resources, the librarian may suggest individuals and organizations you might include in your networking activities, such as a local employment agency, executive search firm, or consulting firm that gathers salary information. You should also consult the standard reference indexes that will give you access to hundreds of journals, magazines, newspapers, newsletters, and reports relevant to jobs and salaries: *Readers' Guide to Periodical Literature, Standard Periodical Directory,* and *Business Periodicals Index.* Many libraries also have computerized reference systems that enable you to quickly research numerous journals, magazines, and newspapers for articles on jobs and salaries. If you've not used these systems before, this is a good time and place to quickly learn what is a basic and essential research tool for gathering this type of information. A little time and effort in learning how to use these resources will more than pay for itself when it comes time to negotiate salary, and you have the information necessary to strike the best deal possible.

3. *Contact professional associations and employment specialists.* Most professional associations and numerous employment firms conduct yearly salary surveys. Again, your local library should have the key directories – *Encyclopedia of Associations* and *National Trade and Professional Associations* -- which provide contact information on all major associations. They should also have directories to employment and executive search firms that might have salary survey information.

4. *Talk to people in your expanding network.* Once you have gathered preliminary salary information from published sources, talk to people who have information on salary ranges for the types of jobs that interest you. This involves the process of networking for information, advice, and referrals. One of the best approaches is to conduct a research project on salary ranges by telephoning personnel offices and asking for assistance with your research. Begin by mentioning that you are conducting research on salary ranges and would appreciate their assistance. In exchange for their cooperation, tell them *"I'll share my research findings with you."* Since many personnel offices are interested in current comparative salary information, they may be happy to share this information with you. If you conclude your telephone interview with the referral question *"Whom else would you suggest I contact for similar information?"*, you should receive additional names and telephone numbers of people who are *"in the know"* about the salaries that interest you. Within a few hours, you should have a good idea of current salary ranges. But be sure to call back or write a nice thank-you letter in which you share you research findings with your informants. Not only is this the proper thing to do, it provides these people with useful information for their own decision-making. Another

approach is to call employment offices, executive search firms, headhunters, career planning offices, and career counselors and ask them if they have any information on such salaries or if they can recommend anyone who might. While these are secondary sources, since they are one or two steps removed from the personnel offices who have the most accurate information, many of these informants will have a fairly accurate picture of current salary ranges. A final approach, which we discussed earlier, involves asking about salaries during your informational interviews. An advantage of these sources is that you get salary information applicable to your geographical area.

5. *Set a dollar figure on your value:* While you arrive at a realistic market value figure by examining comparative salary information, you may also want to set an arbitrary salary figure that you believe you are worth. This arbitrary decision may help guide you toward acquiring new skills and seeking higher level jobs.

DOCUMENT YOUR PERFORMANCE

If you verbally emphasize the importance of performance in determining compensation, you must first document your performance. Documentation gives you the necessary supports for justifying what you're worth.

You should document both your past and present performance by keeping records on your achievements. Your past achievements should be documented as part of your self-assessment -- one of the first things you should have done in your job search. If you did not complete this critical step at that time, better late than never. One of best ways to do this is to complete the form on page 54. Make at least 10 copies of this form. Complete the questions for each of 10 major achievements related to your previous work. This exercise helps you identify your *motivated abilities* which are also your *strengths*. When focusing on achievements relevant to particular jobs and employers, your motivated abilities and strengths become your *performance*. By addressing the questions in this form, you detail each of your achievements around employer's major concerns. If, for example, an employer asks you during the interview *"What are your major strengths?"*, you will be prepared to detail at least 10 strengths that also explain your past performance. You should do more than just list 10 discrete activities you engaged in that demonstrate some degree of performance. Indeed, if you go

---

YOUR ACHIEVEMENTS

INSTRUCTIONS: Prioritize what you believe are your most important achievements in your worklife. An achievement is anything you enjoyed doing, felt you did well, developed a sense of satisfaction, accomplishment, and pride in doing. Make 10 copies of this form and complete one form for each achievement. Focus on only the achievements that relate to previous jobs and employers.

ACHIEVEMENT # ___ : _____

_____

1. How did I get involved? _____

_____

_____

2. What did I do? _____

_____

_____

_____

3. How did I do it? _____

_____

_____

_____

_____

4. What did I especially enjoy about doing it? __

_____

_____

_____

_____

5. Who benefited how from what I did? _____

_____

_____

_____

6. How was I recognized and rewarded? _____

_____

_____

_____

one step further and synthesize all of these achievements into two. or three common strengths, you should be able to communicate a picture of past performance that also constitutes a *pattern* for predicting future performance. Much of the information you generate from this exercise should also appear on your resume.

You should also document your present performance as well as prepare to continue doing so in the future by keeping records of your accomplishments. While you and your employer may complete a standardized performance appraisal form for this purpose, you should go one step further in keeping a *performance diary* that details your accomplishments. Again, avoid the tendency to list duties and responsibilities that are on-going activities related to your job. Instead, you want to emphasize *outcomes* and *benefits* from your performance. Include the following categories of information in your performance diary:

PERFORMANCE DIARY

1. **Date:** _____

2. **What did I accomplish:** _____

   _____

   _____

3. **Who was involved:** _____

   _____

   _____

4. **Who or what benefited from what I did:** _____

   _____

   _____

5. How did I communicate this accomplishment to my supervisor?

_____

_____

_____

CALCULATE YOUR VALUE
AND YOUR SALARY RANGE

Once you know the average salary range for a position, you can calculate a rough estimate of your value for a position. Use the following formula for computing your value:

——CALCULATING YOUR SALARY——
AND SALARY RANGE

1. The average salary or mid-point of the salary range for the position (this figure is based on your research): $ _____

2. Your most recent or present salary: $ _____

3. Subtotal (add the two figures and divide by 2): $ _____

4. Multiple by 15% (.15 x the figure in Item 3): $ _____

5. Add Items 3 and 4; this is your estimated value for the position: $ _____

6. Salary range: calculate plus
   and minus 15% of the figure
   in Item 5:

   $ _____ to $ _____

If, for example, you know the salary range for the position is
$25,000 to $40,000 (average is $32,500) and your current salary is
$27,000 per year, based on this formula, your estimated value for
this position should be $34,250. Your salary range (Item 6) for the
position would be $29,750 to $39,387.

By calculating salary in this manner, you should be able to get
a clear picture of your current market value. Furthermore, your
calculations should be similar to those of the employer. One
important result of this exercise should be reaching some common
statistical ground from which to negotiate your salary. At the same
time, you must factor in the value of your past achievements. Were
you adequately compensated for the level of your performance? If
not, perhaps you need to increase your multiple in Item 4 by 10
percent – from 15 percent to 25 percent. Unless you especially
dislike your present job, a move to another job should result in at
least a 15 percent increase in salary -- but preferably a 20 to 30
percent increase.

BE PREPARED

Whatever you do, make sure you know what both the position
and you are worth. One of the best ways to kill your financial
future is by being both unprepared and unrealistic about your
future salary when asked about your *"salary requirements"* or *"salary
expectations"*.

If you conduct your own salary survey as suggested in this
chapter, you will quickly be on the road to salary success. You will
be prepared to clearly communicate to employers that you are
worth a salary commensurate with your salary expectations. You'll
be able to address the two key salary considerations of the
employer – the value of the position both within and outside the

organization and your salary history -- as well as focus on what should become the most important ingredient in the salary calculation – your potential performance in adding value to the employer's organization and operations.

*One of the best ways to kill
your financial future is
by being both unprepared
and unrealistic about
your future salary.*

Chapter Five

RULES FOR SUCCESS

Why are some people more successful with their job search and salary negotiations than others? Are they more intelligent or talented than others? Do they know something about the job search and how to approach employers that others don't? Is there something about them that inclines them to achieve their salary goals more than others?

Over the years we have learned that successful people do indeed do things differently from others. They aren't necessarily more intelligent nor talented than others. But they are smart in how they approach situations and people. If you want to be successful at both finding a job and achieving your salary goals, you must orient yourself to success. This means taking certain actions that result in clearly communicating your value to employers.

ORIENT YOURSELF TO JOB SEARCH SUCCESS

Job search success is determined by more than just a good plan getting implemented. It is not predetermined nor is it primarily achieved by intelligence, thinking big, time management, or luck. Based upon experience, theory, research, and common sense, we believe you will achieve job search success by following many of these 20 principles:

PRINCIPLES FOR
JOB SEARCH SUCCESS

1. *You should work hard at finding a job:* Make this a daily endeavor and involve your family. Spend the necessary time conducting research on organizations offering job opportunities as well as networking amongst those that are of most interest to you.

2. *You should not be discouraged with set-backs:* You are playing the odds, so expect disappointments and handle them in stride. You will get many *"no's"* before finding the one *"yes"* which is right for you. If you are unable to deal with rejections as part of the game, you will be headed for trouble. Try to turn negatives into positives. Learn from them, leave them, but remember them as stepping stones to future acceptances.

3. *You should be patient and persevere:* Expect three to six months of hard work before you connect with the job that's right for you.

4. *You should be honest with yourself and others:* Honesty is always the best policy, but don't be naive and stupid by confessing your negatives and shortcomings to others.

5. *You should develop a positive attitude toward yourself and others:* Nobody wants to employ guilt-ridden people with inferiority complexes. At the same time, neither do they want to hire self-centered individuals. Focus on your positive characteristics as well as the employer's needs.

6. *You should associate with positive and successful people:* Finding a job largely depends on how well you relate to others and how effectively you network within the job market. Avoid associating with negative and depressing people who complain and have a *"you-can't-do-it"* attitude. Run with winners who have a positive *"can-do"* outlook on life.

7. *You should set goals:* You should have a clear idea of what you want and where you are going. Without these, you will present a confusing and indecisive image to others. Clear goals help direct your job search into productive channels. Setting high goals also will help make you work hard in getting what you want.

8. *You should plan:* Convert your goals into action steps that are organized as short, intermediate, and long-range plans. You should operationalize these plans so they can be realistically implemented.

9. *You should get organized:* Translate your plans into activities, targets, names, addresses, telephone numbers, and materials. Develop an efficient and effective filing system and use a large calendar for setting time targets and recording appointments and useful information.

10. *You should be a good communicator:* Take stock of your oral, written, and nonverbal communication skills. How well do you communicate? Since most aspects of your job search involves communicating with others, and communication skills are one of the most sought-after skills, always present yourself well both verbally and nonverbally.

11. *You should be energetic and enthusiastic:* Employers are attracted to positive people. They don't like negative and depressing people who toil at their work. Generate enthusiasm both verbally and

nonverbally. Check on your telephone voice -- it may be less enthusiastic than your voice in face-to-face situations.

12. *You should ask questions:* Your best information comes from asking questions. The questions you ask helps direct communication with employers. Indeed, the solution to many problems lies in how you frame the question. Learn to develop intelligent questions that are non-aggressive, polite, and interesting to others. Learn to direct conversations around your agenda by asking the right questions. But don't ask too many questions.

13. *You should be a good listener:* Being a good listener is often more important than being a good questioner or talker. Learn to improve your face-to-face listening behavior (nonverbal cues) as well as remember and use information gained from others. Try to make others feel they enjoy talking with you -- you are one of the few people who actually *listens* to what they say.

14. *You should be polite, courteous, and thoughtful:* Treat gatekeepers, especially receptionists and secretaries, like human beings. Avoid being aggressive or too assertive. Try to be polite, courteous, and gracious. Your social graces are being observed. Remember to send thank-you letters -- a very thoughtful thing to do in a job search. Even if rejected, thank employers for the *"opportunity"* given to you. After all, they may later have additional opportunities. A thank-you letter helps them remember you for future reference.

15. *You should be tactful:* Watch what you say to others about other people and your background. Don't be a gossip, back-stabber, or confessor.

16. *You should maintain a professional stance:* Be

neat in what you do and wear, and speak with the confidence and maturity of a professional.

17. *You should demonstrate your intelligence and competence:* Present yourself as someone who gets things done and achieves results -- a *producer*. Employers generally seek people who are bright, hard working, responsible, can communicate well, have positive personalities, maintain good interpersonal relations, are likeable, observe dress and social codes, take initiative, are talented, possess expertise in particular areas, use good judgment, are cooperative, trustworthy, and loyal, generate confidence and credibility, and are conventional. In other words, they like people who score in the *"excellent"* to *"outstanding"* categories of the annual performance evaluation. Many want God!

18. *You should not overdo your job search:* Don't engage in overkill and bore everyone with your *"job search"* stories. Achieve balance in everything you do. Occasionally take a few days off to do nothing related to your job search. Develop a system of incentives and rewards -- such as two free days a week, if you accomplish targets A, B, C, and D.

19. *You should be open-minded and keep an eye open for "luck":* Too much planning can blind you to unexpected and fruitful opportunities. You should welcome serendipity. Learn to re-evaluate your goals and strategies. Seize new opportunities if they appear appropriate.

20. *You should evaluate your progress and adjust:* Take two hours once every two weeks and evaluate what you are doing and accomplishing. If necessary, tinker with your plans and reorganize your activities and priorities. Don't become too routinized and thus kill creativity and innovation.

While these principles specifically apply to organizing and implementing a job search that leads to a job offer, several of the following principles are more applicable to salary negotiations. These are equally valid for individuals who are negotiating salary as part of the job offer or approaching an employer for a raise or renegotiating the terms of employment.

You can price yourself too low and thus communicate that you have little value.

VALUE YOURSELF APPROPRIATELY

Knowing what you are worth and communicating it to employers can be difficult if you price yourself too high or too low. If you are too high, employers may view you as either unrealistic or over-qualified given the structure of their compensation system. On the other hand, you can price yourself too low and thus communicate that you have little value; you are probably under-qualified for the job. The notion that pricing yourself low will give you a better chance at getting and keeping a job is largely a myth. If you under-value yourself, you may not receive the respect you need in order to do a good job. You can give yourself additional value in the eyes of many employers if you price yourself above the norm -- but not too much above it.

DOCUMENT YOUR VALUE

Negotiating techniques are only as good as the information you bring to the negotiations. You will need to justify why you feel you are worth what you say you are worth. More importantly, you must address any objections employers may have to paying you more than what they feel you are worth as well as the amount already budgeted for the position. The best way to do this is to document your achievements and communicate your past achievements as strong indicators of your future performance which will be above the norm. This involves carefully going through the process of knowing what you are worth as outlined in Chapter Four. You might reformulate your documentation into a checklist of *"10 Reasons Why I Should Be Given a Salary of $ _____ a Year."*

USE SUPPORTS

When you make statements about your accomplishments and productivity, try to back them up with *supports*. While documentation is the basis for developing supports (Chapter Four), supports come in many different forms and involve several techniques of persuasion. Can you give an *example* of how you improved production on your last job? Can you *describe* the sales campaign that won you the Best-Copywriter-of-the-Year Award? Can you *compare* the previous bookkeeping system with the one you instituted that saved your last or present employer so much money? When you back up your assertions with supports, you gain several advantages over individuals who do not. Supports help clarify your comments; help substantiate them; help the listener recall them at a later time; and they add interest. You should use a variety of supports in the process of persuading the employer that you are indeed worth what you say you are. Supports include such things as:

- examples
- illustrations
- descriptions
- definitions
- statistics
- comparisons
- testimonials

Use such supports in stressing your accomplishments which are the basis for communicating your value to employers.

PROJECT AN IMAGE
OF VALUE AND SUCCESS

Whether you are conducting a job search or performing on the job, always project an image of success that is equivalent to your expected value. During the job search, your image is projected in your resumes, letters, application forms, networking activities, informational interviews, and job interviews. You must write first-class resumes and letters. When networking and interviewing, you must dress appropriately for the type of position you are seeking. Your use of language and the types of questions you ask must communicate your value.

---

*Always project an image of success
that is equivalent to your
expected value.*

People who command high salaries tend to communicate an *image of class* which is expressed in the quality of their apparel, grooming, nonverbal behaviors, questions, answers, speech, and follow-up behavior. Indeed, your nonverbal behaviors may be more important in justifying your salary requirements than what you say in a salary negotiation session. If you are renegotiating your compensation with your present employer, it's especially important that you have been continuously projecting an image of value and success while on the job.

INVEST THE EMPLOYER'S
TIME IN YOU

The use of time is very important when negotiating salary. Try to invest as much of the employer's time in you as possible. You will have value to the employer as you use up more of his or her time. The best way to do this is to keep the salary question to the very end of the job interview(s). However, should the employer raise the question of salary at the beginning of the application process or during the initial job interview, try to keep your response to the very last job interview. You do this by saying something to this effect:

> *I'm open at present. But I really need to know more about this position and your organization as well as what others with my qualifications normally make. If you don't mind, I'd prefer discussing this matter later, after we've had a chance to address several important questions about the job and how I might best fit into your organization.*

Indeed, the whole purpose of the application process and a series of job interviews should be to exchange information about the value of both the job and you. You want to communicate your value to the employer *before* finally translating your value into a specific salary figure. The employer does not know your value until after he or she has invested time in getting answers to several questions about your achievements and performance. Answers to these questions are not found in resumes, letters, and application forms. Therefore, the answer to the salary question should always take place at the very *end* of your last interview, just prior to being offered the job or accepting it contingent upon reaching agreement on compensation.

ASK AND ANSWER
QUESTIONS INTELLIGENTLY

You must be prepared to give positive answers and ask intelligent questions relevant to compensation. Most employers will ask you about your salary history and salary requirements. If your past salaries were low in comparison to the position in question, you will need to explain why you should be compensated at a much higher rate than in your last position. If your salary requirements are much higher than expected, the employer is likely to object to paying you above the range set for the position. Thus, you will need to respond to the two most common objections:

- *That's more than others with similar qualifications and experience make.*

- *We're not budgeted to pay that much.*

At the same time, you need to ask intelligent questions about the position, company, and employer that will help you make the best decisions possible. For example, what type of pay system operates within this organization? Is compensation tied to performance criteria? If so, what exactly is the criteria and how is it uniformly applied to employees? Does an annual performance appraisal determine pay increases, and how does it operate in practice? What have been the average annual salary increments during the past five years, especially for the position you are considering? Are these primarily cost-of-living increases? What about such benefits as health insurance, child care, education and training, and retirement? How are they structured? How much do employees contribute to the plans? In other words, you should talk about the *details* of compensation rather than deal with salary and benefits in general terms. After all, it's the details that will give you problems once you accept a position and discover that the so-called attractive compensation looked most attractive on paper rather than in practice. In the process of doing so, you again demonstrate your value to employers who, in turn, will respect you more for your knowledge of the employment process.

TAKE NOTES
DURING NEGOTIATIONS

While it is best to memorize what you want to talk about concerning compensation, it's not always possible to remember everything you need to at such an important meeting. Feel free to take notes during the negotiation session as well as bring notes with you that outline issues and questions you need to address with the employer. Especially when you address the question of benefits, it's a good idea to have a checklist of the various types of benefits you expect and notes about the details on each benefit. While some employers may not have answers to each of these questions, by preparing in this manner you at least impress upon the employer that the content of the compensation package is important to you, that you want to be rewarded for performance, and that compensation will be an on-going issue with you rather than something that is only settled at the job offer stage. Again, you increase your value in the eyes of most employers by approaching the salary negotiations in such a manner.

You want to approach the question of compensation from the employer's perspective rather than from one of need, greed, or gamesmanship.

BE REALISTIC AND SEEK COMMON GROUND

You want to approach the question of compensation from the employer's perspective rather than from one of need, greed, or gamesmanship. Keep in mind that most employers have problems they need to solve by hiring new employees. Paying an employee a few hundred or thousand dollars more than expected is really not a major problem for most employers, if they know they will get better value for their money. However, keep in mind that some employers have little flexibility with their pay systems which are often rigidly structured around base pay. You need to sense whether the employer has more flexibility with salary or benefits and negotiate accordingly.

Conventional wisdom suggests that benefits are generally standard and hence one should concentrate on negotiating salary. But in some instances, salary may be fixed -- or at least a ceiling on salary for the position is in place. In these situations, there may be some leeway on the benefits side. For example, we know individuals in education administration -- an area where there are caps on salary ranges -- knowing they were being offered the top dollar amount which the university could pay for their job slot, bargained for two days off each month during which they could do consulting. At $300 a day, that's an additional $7,200 a year!

Being realistic means knowing what both you and the position are worth and then reaching common ground with the employer on the question of compensation. Needy people tend to take any amount offered just to get the job and avoid stressful questions about money. Greedy people over-estimate their worth by playing a game that no one else sees value in continuing, or winning a game in which they may eventually become the loser. Indeed, many employees who over-value themselves, think they are indispensable to employers, and threaten to quit unless their salary demands are met, are often shown the door as a measure of their true value to employers who know that most employees are replaceable -- and often at lower compensation.

The fastest way to eliminate yourself from consideration or initially create problems on the job is to get greedy during the salary stage and thereby force the employer into making a decision he or she feels uncomfortable about but makes nonetheless in order to get the troublesome hiring process over. Your clever negotiation skills may create ill-will at this crucial juncture of the hiring process. If you leave with a job offer from an employer who does not feel good about acceding to your demands, he or she may keep you under close scrutiny in an effort to justify paying your high price.

A general rule is to know when to stop negotiating and start the job. Reaching common ground and setting the stage for mutual respect and cooperation are more important than the few extra dollars you might be able to wring out of the employer by playing hardball when negotiating salary.

BE THOUGHTFUL AND
DEVELOP POSITIVE RELATIONSHIPS

Every step in the interview process should be focused on setting the stage for being a respected employee. How well you perform in the interview, as well as negotiate your salary, will affect how well you get along on the job. Few employers desire adversarial relationships with their employees. While the employer-employee relationship is instrumental in some respects -- your talent in exchange for money – on the other hand, this relationship also involves mutual respect and admiration. Therefore, you should also develop good personal relations with your employer that go beyond the instrumental monetary bonds that hold you together.

One of the best ways to begin developing this personal relationship is to be thoughtful during the interview and salary negotiation stages by sending thank-you letters. Within 48 hours of completing your first interview, send a nice thank-you letter in which you express your appreciation for the opportunity to interview for the position and stress your continuing interest in the position. An example of such a letter appears in Chapter Nine.

After you receive a firm job offer with the question of compensation settled, send an acceptance thank-you letter in which you reiterate your interest in working with the employer and contributing to the success of his or her operations. This thank-you letter is a thoughtful thing to do that very few new employees ever do. In addition, it helps relieve any doubts that employers may have about hiring you. Best of all, most employers *remember* such thoughtful gestures as they begin developing both personal and professional relationships with their new employees. Such a letter expresses an important *attitude* toward the employer and the job that is of central concern to most employers as they scrutinize new employees during the first 90 days. It's always best to be initially remembered as a thoughtful person rather than just another new employee who will be tested in the months ahead.

Chapter Six

RESPOND APPROPRIATELY
TO ADS AND APPLICATIONS

The question of salary is likely to arise during two different stages of the job search: at the beginning, when completing an application, and toward the end, when interviewing for the job and negotiating the job offer.

Your response to the compensation issue will take different forms. For example, at the application stage you must be prepared to identify in writing both your salary history and salary requirements – your financial past and expected future. During the job interview you may address the same issues, but this time you will do so in reference to the employer's position, pay system, and opportunities for advancement.

How you handle the compensation question at each stage will largely determine if you will proceed to the next stage and eventually receive a firm job offer. The job offer, which includes a compensation package, is the final stage of your job search. This is the point where you should negotiate salary and terms of employment in earnest.

SALARY ISSUES

Let's do first things first. At the very beginning of a job search you must be prepared to deal with four salary-related situations which are most likely to arise prior to a job interview. These include:

• Determining the value of jobs.

• Dealing with requests for information on your salary history.

• Stating your salary requirements.

• Responding to vacancy announcements which identify salary for specific positions.

Each of these situations requires thoughtful responses that should result in leaving the door open for a series of job interviews that eventually lead to a job offer which specifies a compensation package. For example, when you read a vacancy announcement that does not mention salary, how will you know if the position fits within your expected salary range? What might you do to determine the value of the position prior to spending your time applying for what may appear to be a $35,000 a year job but in reality is nothing more than a well written ad for a $15,000 a year job?

At the same time, how will you respond to an ad or an application that asks you to reveal either your salary history or your salary expectations? Will you state a specific figure that might be too high or too low and thus eliminate you from further consideration, or should you disregard this request altogether? And what will you do if you find an ad for a job that states a salary range that may appear too high or too low given your present salary? Should you disregard this job altogether, because it may be above or beneath your qualifications and experience, or should you pursue it nonetheless?

Let's address these questions *before* you get that first telephone call that turns into a screening interview which may lead to the first of two or three job interviews, and a job offer where the question of compensation arises again. For in addressing the salary question at this initial application stage, you will be better prepared to address it over the telephone and in face-to-face interview settings.

DETERMINE THE VALUE OF JOBS

If you browse through the business and classified sections of most Saturday or Sunday newspapers, you will discover hundreds of job listings with revealing information about salaries. Some state a specific salary or salary range whereas others only give information about the job and how to apply. Take, for example, the following ads which appeared in nationwide publications:

TREASURER

Dynamic individual with proven history and ability in real estate and equipment financing, as well as cash management, needed for newly created position. The privately held XXXX group of affiliated companies specialize in both truckload transportation as well as commercial real estate. Send resume and salary requirements in strict confidence to: (mailing address)

HUMAN RESOURCES ASSISTANT

XXXX Group is a dynamic company offering a variety of financial services. We are currently seeking an individual to fill this position in our human resources department. Individual will be responsible for processing employee status changes, enrolling and administering benefits plans, chairing compensation committee and coordinating updates of company administration plans. Qualified applicant must have 1-2 years experience in a human resources environment, strong communication skills. Prior experience or education in compensation and benefits administration strongly desired. Excellent benefits package including dental/vision and free parking. Please send resume with salary history to: (mailing address)

RESEARCH ANALYST

The Marketing Services Department of a prestigious National Trade Association seeks individual to perform analysis and research of electronic industries. Position requires a degree in business or

economics with course work in statistics and at least one year
applicable experience. Candidates must be highly organized, detail
oriented and have strong quantitative and communication skills.
Knowledge of Lotus, Harvard Graphics and WordPerfect desired.
Overtime necessary. This is a non-smoking office. Salary to mid
$20's with excellent benefits. Send resume with salary requirements
to: (mailing address)

While you can easily screen in or out those jobs which mention
salary, other jobs are somewhat of a mystery. Indeed, many ads
may sound like a job pays $40,000 or more, but in reality someone
did a great job writing an attractive ad for a $15,000 a year job.
How much, for example, do you think this job pays?

WAREHOUSE/PRODUCTION

Hardworking individuals needed for quality fabrication/production
work. Training provided. Good references necessary. Must be willing
to work 40 to 50 hours per week. Only those interested in a career
opportunity please apply in person to: (address)

This job actually pays $7.00 an hour or $300 to $400 per week.

Want ads and vacancy announcements that do not provide
information on salaries can be a waste of your time and effort. In
some cases an employer is just *"testing the waters"* by placing an ad
that would generate numerous resumes for future reference. In
other cases the employer has a very broad salary range in mind but
prefers looking at the salary history of candidates prior to committing a narrow salary range to the job. In many of these cases, the
employer lets the market determine his or her salary range.

If you apply for a job which does not reveal a salary range, you
will have to guess what salary is likely to be offered given your
knowledge of jobs and salaries as well as your intuition. How do
you make a *"best guess"* in such a situation? Obviously, you don't
want to be too high nor too low. Neither do you want to waste
time applying for jobs that are beneath your qualifications and
experience. We suggest several approaches to dealing with this
situation:

- *Carefully analyze the listing for salary clues:* Look at
each word and sentence for clues about the salary level
of the position. For example, does the ad state minimum

educational requirements? If the position requires a BA, it should be worth at least $20,000. If the employer wants an MA, price the position at $27,000. Each year of required experience should be worth $2,000 per year for the first five years and $1,000 per year thereafter. Therefore, if the ad states minimum qualifications are a BA and 3 years of progressive experience, price the job at $26,000. If the requirement is an MA and 10 years experience, price the job at $42,000. However, you may need to make some adjustments for regional variations. The baseline value of a BA and MA will differ from region to region. While they may be valued similarly in New York City, Boston, Washington, DC, San Francisco, and Los Angeles, they have different value in Wyoming, Little Rock, and Peoria. Our shorthand method should bring you within 20 percent of the employer's salary range, which is close enough for finding common ground to negotiate.

If the position requires a BA, it should be worth at least $20,000. If the employer wants an MA, price the position at $27,000.

• *Compare other ads that announce similar positions:* If you survey various publications, you should be able to find the same or similar positions with other companies that include salary ranges in the ads. After identifying five such ads, you will have a good idea of the going salary range for such a position.

• *Contact individuals for salary information:* The quickest way to get salary information on the position is to call the personnel office of the company and frankly ask *"What is the salary range for this position?"* In many cases they will tell you. In other cases you won't know the name, address, or telephone number of the company, because you are responding to a blind ad. If this happens, call another company that might have a similar position and ask them if they know what might be the *"going rate"* for this type of position in the industry as a whole as well as in your region.

Perhaps more important than guessing about the salary range for the position is *how* you respond to the ad. Most ads and application forms will request that you state in writing either your salary history or salary requirements. In fact, most employers are especially interested in your salary history because it gives them the most important information for valuing you as well as making you a salary offer which is likely to be no more than a 10 to 20 percent increase over your present or last salary. Whatever you do, beware of how you respond to these questions, because you may create a self-fulfilling prophecy which you will have to live with for many years -- and many paychecks -- to come.

DEAL WITH
YOUR SALARY HISTORY

Regardless of how unfair it may seem, your last or present salary is the most powerful determiner of your next salary. To the surprise of many job seekers and employees, it really doesn't make much difference how important or productive you think you are since employers are not particularly keen about paying new employees more than 15 percent above their past salary and current employees more than 5 percent above last year's salary. Therefore, employers want to know your salary history in order to determine your value. Once they have this information, they will extend a *"reasonable"* job offer. Individuals who do experience a major salary jump -- a 30 to 100 percent increase -- do so because their skills are especially in demand. Most employees seldom experience more than a 10 percent increase in salary.

How, then, do you deal with the question of salary history when you know full well that your answer is likely to become a self-fulling prophecy -- your most recent salary plus 10 to 20 percent?

Here you have several options, from being honest but dumb to lying to the employer.

The *honest but dumb* approach is to state your net salary – your weekly or monthly take-home pay. While you may feel you are being completely honest, at the same time you can't get much dumber than this: you are revealing the very lowest amount of money you receive from a job! Welcome to the world of the salaried disadvantaged.

If you engage in *lying*, the sky is the limit on what you might tell the employer. Unfortunately, this lie may not take you very far, especially when the employer decides to check your earnings with your last employer or ask to see pay stubs for salary verification. While you may be clever enough to get your past employer to also lie as well as create some phony pay stubs, such deception is a high risk approach. Some job applicants may use this approach successfully but chances are you will be *"found out"* and perhaps lose more than a chance at this job.

Begin thinking in terms of total compensation rather than just a base salary which translates your benefits into a salary equivalent figure.

A third approach is to do some *creative, but truthful, calculating* when determining your salary history. Begin thinking in terms of *total compensation*, rather than just a base salary, which translates your benefits into a salary equivalent figure. Indeed, given the flexible benefit packages now offered to many employees, some employees choose to receive many benefits as part of their salary. Since compensation packages are not necessarily equivalent among employers, make sure you are comparing apples with apples rather than apples with oranges. For example, wages may constitute only 60 or 70 percent of total compensation with some employers, but wages may constitute as much as 90 percent of compensation with other employers. A $35,000 a year salary figure with one employer may be equivalent to a $30,000 salary figure with other employers if certain benefits are not included in the compensation package.

Most employers can put a dollar figure on benefits. Depending on what is included in your compensation package, you may want to multiply your gross monthly or yearly salary figure by 30 percent and add that additional amount to your base salary figure. For example, consider the case of an individual who makes $30,000 a year. The creative way to calculate the salary that may also truthfully reflect the individual's total compensation is as follows:

BASE YEARLY/ MONTHLY SALARY	$30,000 a year ($2,500 per month at the beginning of the year but $3,000 per month at the end of the year)
BENEFITS	30% of base salary
COMPENSATION	$39,000

Another approach is to use your highest monthly salary, including any bonuses, as the baseline for calculating a new yearly salary figure. For example, if you made $30,000 last year for an average of $2,500 per month -- but during the last two months you received a raise or additional compensation of $3,000 a month -- use the $3,000 a month as your salary base. Therefore, your so-called $30,000 a year at $2,500 per month looks much lower than $30,000 a year but with a recent increase to $3,000 per month:

YEARLY SALARY BASED ON $3,000 PER MONTH	$36,000

In this case you should tell the employer that you make $3,000 per month or $36,000 a year. Better still, if you factor in an additional 30 percent for benefits, your total compensation picture will be:

```
TOTAL COMPENSATION
BASED ON A $3,000
PER MONTH SALARY                    $46,800
```

Therefore, when you negotiate a salary which will likely be 15 to 20 percent above your present base, you will be talking about a salary close to $50,000. Had you not figured your salary history in this manner, you might be talking closer to $35,000.

A final approach to creatively calculating your salary history is to include additional work-related income in your total salary figure. If, for example, you do outside consulting work and you were lucky enough to make $500 to $1,000 a day on a project, factor this information into your salary figure. But don't be unrealistic by thinking you are worth $500 to $1,000 a day just because you happened to have one lucky day during the past year or two! Use this information as an indicator: you are potentially worth more than your normal salary. In addition, will this new job preclude you from engaging in outside income generating activities or will it allow you to either *"daylight"* or *"moonlight"*?

Educators are a special case in point when dealing with the question of salary history. Contrary to what many educators may think, they actually receive decent salaries for the amount of time they work. The major problem is that their yearly salary is only based upon seven to nine months of work. When figuring their salary history, educators should analyze their salary in terms of the hours, weeks, or months worked rather than a base yearly salary. If, for example, an educator makes $25,000 a year but in reality only works eight months out of the year, their salary is actually $3,125 per month or $37,500 a year. Indeed, many higher educators average $45,000 a year but only work eight months out of the year. In addition, they have liberal opportunities to both *"daylight"* and *"moonlight"*. Such a workload translates into the equivalent of $5,625 per month or $67,500 per year -- not bad for what many claim to be a poorly paid profession!

While some employers may dispute the way in which you calculate your salary history -- since they, too, offer benefits that can be translated into salary equivalents -- they eventually must face up to the fact that you are worth more than what your base salary figure might indicate. Furthermore, they need to translate *their* benefit package into a salary equivalent amount for comparative purposes. The whole point of engaging in such creative salary calculations is to *stress your true value* which is higher than a base wage figure. Moreover, you should be financially rewarded on the basis of performance rather than on the basis of salary history. While you recognize that salary history is an important component in the employer's salary calculations, you are reluctant to accept a salary that is merely based on a 10 to 20 percent increase over your present salary. If you initially deal with the salary history question in this manner, you will begin focusing the main thrust of your job search on how your performance will add value to the employer and the organization. This is exactly the point you want to consistently make from the initial application step to the final job offer stage where you will negotiate the total compensation package in earnest.

Given these different ways of calculating so-called *"salary history"*, it would be dumb to just reveal monthly or yearly take-home pay. Individuals that make this mistake literally commit salary suicide!

Now that you have several alternative ways of calculating your salary history, how should you respond to ads and applications that ask you to reveal your salary history? You have two major alternatives here:

- *Leave this information off altogether in anticipation that you will deal with the question of salary when being interviewed for the job:* While it is always best to leave the salary question to the end -- after you have demon-strated your value to the employee -- this is not always possible. Many employers want to initially deal with the salary question in order to screen candidates in or out of the hiring process. If you don't provide this requested information, the employer may screen you out for having an incomplete application -- you can't follow instructions! If you guess wrong and state too high or too low a salary figure, you may be screened out prematurely. This is one of those proverbial *"Damned if you do, damned if you don't"* situations. We have no best advice here except to examine other alternative ways of responding to the situation.

• *State your salary history:* Make your best calculation based on knowledge of your total compensation as we indicated earlier. State either a monthly or yearly salary figure, whichever is highest. While this response will satisfy the employer's application requirement, it is risky in the sense that you may present too high or too low a figure in reference to the job. If it screens you out, so much the better. You don't want to waste your time with jobs that are above or beneath your qualifications, experience, and salary history. At least your response brings this application to an end so you can concentrate your efforts on other more appropriate jobs.

STATE YOUR SALARY REQUIREMENTS

Other ads and applications will ask you for your salary requirements. Your salary requirements are what you *expect to receive* regardless of what you have made in the past. These are your expectations.

You have a larger range of alternatives with this question than with salary history:

• *Leave this information blank:* Rather than state an expected salary or salary range, don't respond to this question at all. The employer will assume you either forgot to include it or you are *"open"* to the employer's salary range.

• *State "Open" or "Negotiable":* These terms indicate to the employer that you are flexible about salary and willing to negotiate. We prefer this approach to the salary expectation question, because it puts the question off. It gives you a chance to find out more about the position as well as communicate your qualifications to the interviewer. Everything you do between now and when you receive the job offer should be aimed at demonstrating your value to the employer. At the end you will want to translate your value into a specific salary range which will be negotiated into a specific salary figure. The more you can invest the employer's time in you, the better should be your negotiating position. You do this by keeping the salary question to the very last.

Everything you do between now and when you receive the job offer should be aimed at demonstrating your value to the employer.

• *State a salary range:* If you have a good idea of the employer's salary range, indicate your salary range. However, make sure the bottom of your range overlaps with the top of the employer's range. For example, if the employer's range is $27,000 to $32,000, make your range $32,000 to $37,000. This gives you *"common ground"* around which to later negotiate a final salary figure.

RESPOND TO STATED SALARY RANGES

Many employment ads and vacancy announcements will state the salary or salary range for a position. However, the degree to which salary ranges are specified and the extent to which they are negotiable depends on the level and importance of the position. In general, the widest salary ranges are assigned to the most negotiable positions -- high level jobs. The lowest level jobs tend to have fixed salaries assigned to them, and few of these jobs are negotiable. What this means in practice is that if a position is valued under $20,000, the ad will normally state a specific figure, such as $18,250. If the position is valued between $20,000 and $50,000, the ad or announcement often includes a narrow salary range, such as

$35,000 to $40,000. If the position is valued over $50,000, the stated range may be very broad or framed in the ultimate negotiable terms: $60,000+.

A stated range gives you information on whether you want to consider the job as well as indicates that the employer has some flexibility in negotiating salary. How far above the top of the range he or she can negotiate is questionable, especially since many pay systems are relatively rigid. In general, however, employers have little flexibility to negotiate lower level salaries. They have greater flexibility to negotiate salaries for high level positions. After all, top talent is a scarce commodity that must be acquired through flexible compensation policies that enable employers to negotiate what is necessary in order to acquire needed talent.

This salary range information gives you important clues as to how much flexibility you might have in the final negotiation session.

When you apply for a job that has a stated salary range, the employer assumes your salary history and expectations fit into his or her stated range. But your willingness to respond to the ad or vacancy announcement does not necessarily commit you to accepting the employer's salary range. This salary range information gives you important clues as to how much flexibility you might have in the final salary negotiation session. If you make the top of the employer's salary range the bottom of your salary range, you should have some room to negotiate. However, don't expect the employer to have much flexibility beyond the top of the stated salary range. Going beyond the top of the salary range only occurs when employers feel they are hiring an exceptionally qualified and promising candidate.

If, on the other hand, you decide to apply for a job that is beneath or far above your salary history, be prepared to explain why you appear to be either over-qualified or under-qualified for the position. Such questions will eventually surface during the course of job interviews. Again, treat salary ranges as indications of the value of both the position and the employee who will occupy the position. If you are applying for a position that pays much higher than your salary history appears to justify, you will have to explain in detail how you acquired this sudden increase in value!

Chapter Seven

COMMUNICATE YOUR VALUE IN INTERVIEWS

Once you've passed the initial application and screening stages of your job search, the next step is to be interviewed for a job. The interview can take many forms. It may start with a telephone call from the employer who is attempting to screen a pool of 10 possible candidates for identifying three finalists who will be invited to job interviews. If you become one of the finalists, you may actually go through two or three interviews – each being a different type -- before being offered the job and arriving at a mutually satisfactory compensation agreement.

During each stage of the job interview, the question of salary and compensation may arise unexpectedly. For example, as part of the telephone screening interview, the employer may ask you about your salary expectations or salary requirements. If not then, the employer may ask you the same question during the initial interview or during the second or third interview. Whatever the timing and scenario, you must be prepared to respond to the salary question at any time during your job search. For your answer to this one key question can quickly eliminate you from further consideration. A wrong answer can also result in under-valuing you for the position and being offered a salary lower than what you should receive had you been better prepared for the interview.

INTERVIEWING PRINCIPLES

As you prepare for any interview -- be it a job interview or a meeting with your present employer to discuss your performance and future compensation -- keep in mind several principles for asking and answering questions. These principles will help you focus on the most important goal of the interview -- exchanging useful information for making a job decision.

While the major purpose of a resume is to communicate your qualifications to employers, the major purpose of the interview should be to communicate your *value* to employers. In the interview, your qualifications become translated into value which, in turn, is assigned a salary figure. How well you communicate your value in the interview will affect the size of your compensation package.

The major purpose of the interview should be to communicate your value to employers.

Many job hunters feel they need to practice answers to standard interview questions in order to impress interviewers. Indeed, many interview books are filled with examples of questions and answers which readers are urged to practice as well as mimic during interviews. As a result, many interviewees learn to play the role of interviewee. They primarily give *"canned"* answers to interviewer's questions. After a while most interviewees sound the same as they give similar answers to interviewer's questions.

The problem with this approach is that it is a form of role playing that communicates little content or value to employers. Your goal should be to communicate *your value* to employers rather than recite what many people consider to be correct answers to questions. You do this by following certain principles that help you formulate detailed answers and thoughtful questions which also communicate the *"unique you"* to employers.

You communicate your value to employers by the way in which you answer and ask questions. When answering and asking questions, you should try to engage in the following interview behaviors:

- *Focus on your major strengths and accomplishments:* Throughout your job search, and especially during the interview, you should stress your most important qualities -- your skills, strengths, and accomplishments. While employers put people on their payrolls, they are most interested in hiring specific skills that translate into productivity for the organization.

- *Be sufficiently redundant on points that stress your benefits:* A certain level of redundancy is necessary in the interview. While you will cover many different subjects and issues relevant to the job during the interview, you should stress over and over again your major qualifications and central value to the employer. Try to formulate answers that stress your *benefits* in reference to the position, employer, and organization. Employers are looking for benefits from their employees.

Employers are looking for benefits from their employees.

- *Turn potential negatives into positives:* While employers are looking for reasons to hire you, they are also looking for reasons not to hire you. Many will ask questions that are designed to identify your weaknesses or negatives. Other questions are aimed at finding objections to hiring you. For example, the interviewer might ask you some negative questions about your background: *"What are your major weaknesses?"* or *"Why didn't you get better grades in school?"* They may also raise objections to your salary requirements: *"How can I justify paying you this much when others in our organization with similar qualifications and experience are making less?"* Try to respond to these questions with positive answers that again stress your value. For example, your major weakness might be the following:

> *I often get so involved with my work that I neglect my family. I'm learning to better balance my professional and personal lives.*

The reason you didn't get better grades in college might be the following:

> *I had hoped to do better, but I was carrying full course loads, working part-time, and participating 15 hours a week in student government.*

And a positive response to the salary objection might be this:

> *I'm sure inequities exist in most organizations, and it's something employers want to eliminate in their efforts to be fair to all. I feel I should be compensated on the basis of my value and performance, as we've already discussed. Given what you've said about the role of the performance appraisal in determining compensation, I'm pleased that management is committed to rewarding employees according to their performance.*

- *Be a good listener:* The more you can get the interviewer to talk about the position and organization, the better should be your position in the job interview. Listen carefully for clues about the value of the position and compensation policies of the organization. Answer the interviewer's questions in detail and by using positive form, but do appear to be someone who listens attentively. You do this by focusing your attention on the interviewer and what he or she is saying, overlooking irritating mannerisms and comments, withholding evaluations of messages received, and giving positive nonverbal feedback (nod in agreement, smile occasionally, eye contact). Employers appreciate employees who are good listeners. They communicate a certain *attitude* that is welcomed by employers.

- *Be employer-centered rather than self-centered:* While you do want to talk about your accomplishments by using such active verbs as *"I completed"*, *"I directed"*, I *supervised"*, or *"I initiated"*, you must also direct your attention to the employer's needs. Keep in mind that the employer has problems to solve. One problem for which you are interviewing is to find someone to fill a position that solves other problems. The more you can talk in the language of the employer about solving his or her problems, the stronger will be your position in the interview process. Avoid talking about benefits you should receive from the employer until the very end when you negotiate the compensation package. If you talk about salary, vacation time, child care policies, and retirement plans early in the interview, you will communicate the wrong message to the employer -- that you are looking for a place to reap benefits rather than generate additional value for the employer. In other words, analyze your audience *before* addressing issues concerning your qualifications and value.

- *Answer and ask questions directly and in detail:* An interviewer's questions deserve thoughtful, focused, and detailed answers. Avoid simple *"yes"* or *"no"* answers. Each question asked of you should become another opportunity for you to communicate your value to the employer. You cannot do this if you prepare a set of stock role playing answers to standard interview questions that others typically serve up to interviewers. Employers want to know how you can best solve their problems. You communicate your value by explaining exactly what you will do for the employer based on your previous performance as well as your understanding of the position, employer, and organization.

- *Use supports for making your points:* One of the best ways to express your value when providing detailed answers to questions is to use supports. These come in many forms: examples, illustrations, descriptions, definitions, statistics, comparisons, or testimonials. If, for example, you want to communicate to the employer that you helped promote productivity on your last job, don't just state this accomplishment in general terms. Use an example that explains what you did or offer a statistic:

  > *By reorganizing the sales force into five new regional centers, I was able to increase sales by nearly 70 percent over the next 12 month period. This meant an additional $800,000 in profits and a much happier sales force.*

- *Give positive nonverbal clues and feedback:* Over 60 percent of what is communicated is done nonverbally. How you dress, sit, listen, smell, use eye contact, shake hands, and eat may be more important than how you respond verbally to questions. Be sure your nonverbal behaviors, especially your dress and appearance, are appropriate for the position. For example, if you are interviewing for a position that pays $30,000 or more a year, dress like you are worth every penny of that salary -- if not more. When asked about salary and the employer's salary range, make sure your nonverbal responses are consistent with your verbal response. Don't nod your head in agreement while you are saying you were thinking of a higher salary. Such nonverbal behavior contradicts your verbal behavior and thus may raise questions about your honesty in dealing with the employer.

- *Help the interviewer through the process:* Contrary to what many interviewees may think, not all interviewers are experts in conducting job interviews and negotiating salaries. For many, the interview is an intrusion into their important day-to-day job routines. Not surprisingly, many interviewers do not ask the most important questions or they fail to follow-through on others. The

more you can help the interviewer get through this
process, the better should be your position with the
interviewer. If, for example, the interviewer forgets to ask
about your major achievements, you might volunteer this
question in the form of an observation relevant to the
position by mentioning that your experience seems to
have prepared you well for this position. You should
then detail your relevant accomplishments as they relate
to the position. Keep with you a list of pertinent points
you want to make regarding your qualifications as well
as questions you need to ask the interviewer. If you fail
to remember all of them, near the end of the interview
you should mention to the interviewer that you have a
few questions you wanted to ask and wrote them down
so you would be sure to ask them. Then refer to your
list as you ask questions you need answered or stress
your accomplishments so you can best communicate your
value to the employer.

INITIATING THE
SALARY QUESTION

Who should initiate the question of compensation? As any
negotiating expert will tell you, it's always preferable to have the
other person expose his or her hand first so you will have some
idea of the other person's negotiating parameters and the base or
ranges from which you are operating in reference to the other
person. Ideally, you want the employer to reveal early on in the
interview something to this effect: *"For your information, the salary
range for this position is $32,000 to $36,500."*
However, few employers are this up-front during the interview.
Instead, they want you to expose your hand first by asking you
one of two questions, or both: *"What are your salary expectations for
this position? What are you making at present?"* Somewhere during the
interviews, both of you will have to answer each other's question.
But who goes first may be critical to the final salary outcome.
The major principle you should follow for addressing the salary
question is to try to *neutralize* it until the very last interview,
which should be the interview where you are extended a job offer

contingent upon reaching a satisfactory compensation agreement. The reason you want to do this is very simple: the two-fold purpose of your job search, especially the job interview, has been to communicate your qualifications to employers and determine whether the job is right for you. When addressing the issue of compensation, qualifications mean your value as translated into salary and benefits. If you prematurely address the compensation question by discussing dollars and cents prior to communicating your value to the employer, you will commit a serious error in judgment: both you and the employer have decided on price *before* looking at the product. Chances are you will decide on a low price since few employers are about to pay a high price at this stage of the hiring process.

Try to neutralize the salary questions until the very last interview.

But there are practical limitations to what extent you will be successful in neutralizing the compensation issue. After all, employers have an interest in learning as soon as possible about your salary history and salary requirements. Therefore, you must be prepared to answer the employer's questions about compensation early in the interview. The best way to neutralize such questions is to respond (with some variation) in the following manner:

> *If you don't mind, I would prefer giving you a specific answer after I've had a chance to learn more about the position and your organization. I'm sure we can reach mutual agreement on that issue at that time.*

While this is a good response for neutralizing the employer's question, you should also take the employer's question as an opportunity to learn more about the position and organization. In other words, you want to do more than neutralize this question by pushing it off until the very last interview. This is a good time to turn what is potentially a sensitive and inappropriate question for you into an important employer-initiated opener into a whole series of important questions concerning the value of the position and the internal personnel policies of the organization. Take this question as an opportunity to learn more about the employer. This is a good question from which to initiate a detailed discussion for valuing the position. For example, you might ask several of these questions:

- *What are the duties and responsibilities assigned to this position?*

- *Does it involve extensive travel and overtime?*

- *Whom would I be working with, and how many people might I be supervising?*

- *Whom would I report to?*

- *How does your organization structure its pay system, personnel policies, and promotions as well as dispense rewards?*

- *Is performance important for compensation increases and promotions or is seniority a key factor?*

- *How does the performance appraisal operate in terms of rewarding individual and group performance?*

- *What are some of the problems the previous individuals experienced on this job in terms of responsibilities, people, and performance?*

By responding to the compensation question in this manner, you indicate to the employer that you have important questions that go to the heart of the position and organization. You need to know more about the position, employer, and organization before you can seriously talk about money. Employers understand the importance of these questions and will respect you for such a response. Above all, you indicate that you are a serious candidate who needs to learn more about the position and organization before making an employment decision. A response that moves the discussion to key compensation issues is much more impressive to employers than a delaying tactic used by clever negotiators to put the salary question off to the end of the interview.

ANSWERING THE QUESTION

Delaying the salary question to the very end is not always possible nor practical given the demands placed on you by some interviewers. When the salary question arises -- assuming you cannot or do not want to put it off until later -- you should do one of two things. First, you can turn the question around by asking *"What is the salary range for this position?"* or *"How much is budgeted?"* or *"How much would someone with my qualifications and experience receive in this position?"*

A second response is more forthcoming and directly addresses the salary issue. Your first step should be to clearly *summarize* the job duties and responsibilities as you understand them. At this point you are attempting to do two things:

- Seek clarification from the interviewer as to the actual job and all it involves.

- Emphasize the level of skills required in the most positive way. In other words, you emphasize the value and worth of this position to the organization and subtly this may help support the actual salary figure that the interviewer or you later provide.

You might do this, for example, by saying,

> As I understand it, I would report directly to the vice-president in charge of marketing, and I would have full authority for marketing decisions that involved expenditures of up to $50,000. I would have a staff of five people -- a secretary, two copywriters, and two marketing assistants.

Such a summary statement establishes for both you and the interviewer that (1) this position reports to the highest levels of authority; (2) this position is responsible for decision-making involving fairly large sums of money; and (3) this position involves supervision of staff.

Although you may not explicitly draw the connection, you are emphasizing the value of this position to the organization. This position should be worth a lot more than one in which the hiree will report to the marketing manager, be required to get approval for all expenditures over $100, and has no staff -- just access to the secretarial pool! By doing this, you will focus the salary questions (that you have not yet responded to) around the exact work you must perform on the job in exchange for salary and benefits. You have also seized the opportunity to focus on the value of the person. who will be selected to fill this vacancy.

Your conversation might go something like this. The employer poses the question:

What are your salary requirements?

Your first response should be to summarize the responsibilities of the position:

*Let me see if I understand all that is involved with this position and job. I would be expected to _____
_____. Have I covered everything or are there some other responsibilities I should know about?*

This response focuses the salary question around the value of the position in relation to you. After the interviewer responds to your final question, answer the initial salary expectation question in this manner:

What is the normal range in your company for a position such as this?

This question establishes the value as well as the range for the *position or job* -- two important pieces of information you need before proceeding further into the salary negotiation stage. The employer normally will give you the requested salary range. Once he or she does, depending on how you feel about the figure, you can follow up with one more question:

What would be the normal salary range for someone with my qualifications?

This question further establishes the value for the *individual* versus the position. This line of questioning will yield the salary expectations of the employer without revealing your desired salary figure or range. It also will indicate whether the employer distinguishes between individuals and positions when establishing salary figures.

At this stage you are prepared to state your expected salary. You can either state a specific figure or a salary range. As we will see in the next chapter, when we examine the negotiation process, it's preferable to state a range. Your best strategy is to place the top of the employer's range at the bottom of your range. This gives you common ground from which to negotiate the final offer. If you do this, you should be able to increase your salary above the employer's norm.

QUESTIONS YOU NEED TO ANSWER

During the job interview you will be asked numerous questions about your education, work experience, career goals, and personality. At this point most interviewers have already decided that you have the necessary skills to perform the job. What they are most interested in is meeting you in person to determine if you will *"fit in"* with their organization. They want to know what kind of person you are. What about your attitudes, motivations, and goals in relation to work, employers, and your future? Are you the type of person who is likely to get along well with others in the organization? How do you dress and interact socially with others? Employers also want to settle the question of compensation if they decide to offer you the job. While they prefer that you accept what they initially offer you, employers also expect to negotiate salary and benefits.

You can expect the interviewer will ask you several of these questions in the process of determining your value:

ANTICIPATED QUESTIONS

Education

- *Describe your educational background.*
- *Why did you attend _____ University (or College)?*
- *Why did you major in _____?*
- *What was your grade point average?*
- *What subjects did you enjoy the most? The least? Why?*
- *What leadership positions did you hold?*
- *How did you finance your education?*
- *If you started all over, what would you change about your education?*
- *Why were your grades so low? So high?*
- *Did you do the best you could in school? If not, why not?*

Work Experience

- *What were your major achievements in each of your past jobs?*
- *Why did you change jobs before?*
- *What do you most enjoy doing?*
- *What did you like about your boss? Dislike?*
- *Which job did you enjoy the most? Why?*
- *Which job did you enjoy the least? Why?*
- *Have you ever been fired? Why?*
- *What skills will you bring to this job?*

Career Goals

- *What ideally would you like to do?*
- *Why are you looking for another job?*
- *What ideally would you like to do?*
- *Why should we hire you?*
- *What do you want to be doing five years from now?*
- *What are your short-range and long-range career goals?*
- *What other types of jobs are you considering? Other companies?*

Personal Considerations

- *Tell me about yourself.*
- *What are you major weaknesses? Your major strengths?*
- *What causes you to lose your temper?*
- *What do you do in your spare time? Do you have any hobbies?*
- *What types of books do you read?*
- *What role does your family play in your career?*
- *How well do you work under pressure? In meeting deadlines?*
- *Tell me about your management philosophy.*
- *How much initiative do you take?*
- *What types of types of people do you prefer working with?*
- *How ____ (creative, analytical, tactful, etc.) are you?*
- *If you could change your life, what would you do differently?*
- *Who are your references?*

Judgment

- *Why do you want to join our organization?*
- *Why do you think you are qualified for this position?*
- *How would you improve our operations?*
- *What attracted you to our company?*
- *If you could choose your job and organization, where would you go?*

Compensation

- *What are you making at present?*
- *How much were you making on your last job?*
- *What are your salary requirements?*
- *What is the lowest pay you will take?*
- *How much do you think you are worth for this job?*
- *Why should we pay you more than others in our organization who have similar qualifications and experience?*
- *How much do you want to be making five years from now?*

Anticipate these as well as other questions the interviewer might ask so you can prepare well thought-out responses prior to the interview. It is far easier to formulate positive responses to interview questions in the relaxed setting of your living room than in the stressful and time constrained setting of the job interview.

QUESTIONS YOU SHOULD ASK

As you prepare for the interview, you also should outline questions you want to ask the prospective employer. You need to ask questions to elicit information *you* need about the position and organization; indeed, you want to know if the position is fit for you. In addition, your interests, qualifications, personality, and competence will be partly judged by the number and types of questions you ask the interviewer. By the very act of asking intelligent questions, you give yourself additional value in the eyes of employers.

What types of questions should you ask in order to get information about the job as well as impress the interviewer about your value? In general, questions relating to job duties, responsibilities, opportunities for training, and employee advancement within the company are appropriate. Avoid asking self-centered questions during initial interviews or early stages of the interview unless they are raised first by the interviewer. Of course you are interested in salary, but you do not want to create the impression it is your primary concern. Remember, your prospective employer is interested in what *benefits* you will bring to the organization. At the same time, you need to *establish your value* in the eyes of the employer prior to discussing money.

The following set of questions outline some of the most common questions interviewees should ask:

YOUR QUESTIONS

- *What duties and responsibilities does this job entail?*
- *Where does this position fit into the organization?*
- *Is this a new position?*
- *What kind of person are you looking for?*
- *When was the last person promoted?*
- *What is the best experience and background for this position?*
- *Whom would I report to? Tell me a little about these people.*
- *Are you happy with them? What are their strengths and*

weaknesses?
- *What are your expectations for me?*
- *May I talk with present and previous employees about this job and organization?*
- *What problems might I expect to encounter on this job? (efficiency, quality control, declining profits, internal politics, evaluation)*
- *What has been done recently in regards to _____?*
- *What is the normal pay range for this job?*
- *How are raises and promotions determined in this organization?*
- *How did you get your job?*
- *How long have you been with this company?*
- *Tell me about promotions and advancement with your company.*
- *What might I expect for myself?*

By formulating questions prior to the interview, you demonstrate concern about the position as well as preparation for the interview. Interviewers should view you in a positive manner for doing this.

USE POSITIVE FORM

The way you phrase your questions and answers can be as important as the actual content of your communication when communicating your value to employers. What you want to achieve is *positive form*. This means avoiding negatives by presenting yourself in as positive a light as possible. In the interview, several opportunities arise for enhancing your image through the use of positive form.

The first use of positive form relates to *names*. Each of us likes to be called by our name. Make sure you get the name of the interviewer, get it right, and use it from time to time as you speak. Use the interviewer's title (Miss, Mrs., Mr., Dr., Professor, etc.) and last name. Never call the interviewer by his or her first name unless specifically requested to do so -- even if the interviewer uses your first name. Many interviewers will be offended by such familiarity.

A second use of positive form is inherent in the *way you phrase questions and answers.* For example, rather than ask *"What are the duties of _____ position?"*, ask *"What would be my duties?"* This form of questioning subtly plants the positive thought of you in the position. This is not presumptuous because you use the word *"would"*, which indicates you are not overly sure of yourself.

A third use of positive form relates to *good grammar.* Proper use of language is not something to be left in the English classroom. Many so-called *"educated"* people do not use good grammar, and many of these people do not interview successfully. Check your use of grammar. If it is not impeccable, make an effort to improve it before the interview.

Fourth, use *good diction.* One of the most common problems is to shorten words. How many people do you hear say *"goin"* instead of *"going"*, or *"gonna"* rather then *"going to"*? Another problem is substituting, eliminating, or adding on consonants: *"Adlanta"* rather than *"Atlanta"*, *"din't"* rather than *"didn't"*, *"idear"* rather than *"idea"*. Do you do this? Do you ever say *"yea"* rather the *"yes"*? The use of sloppy speech is a habit many people -- including the well educated -- get into. But it is a habit -- a learned and reinforced behavior -- you can change. If you have a tendency to modify words these in manners, it is a habit worth correcting.

Fifth, avoid using *vocalized pauses.* An occasional silence is acceptable and preferable to overuse of *"ahs"* and *"uhms"*. Try not to fill silences with *"ah"* or *"and ah"*. Vocalized pauses distract the listener from your message and the excessive use can be annoying.

Sixth, avoid the use of *fillers.* Fillers add no information and, if overdone, also distract the listener. The most commonly used fillers are *"you know"*, *"like"* and *"okay"*. If used frequently, the listener becomes distracted and will find it hard to concentrate on the content of your message.

Seventh, use *active verbs.* When talking about what you have done or will do, active verbs like *"organized"*, *"analyzed"*, or *"supervised"* are preferable to the nouns *"organizer"*, *"analyst"*, or *"supervisor"*. Even stronger action words can be used to indicate your present strengths: *"organize"*, *"analyze"*, and *"supervise"*. Avoid the passive voice. For example, instead of saying *"The entire conference was organized by me"* (passive), say *"I organized the entire conference"* (active).

Eighth, avoid using *tentative, indecisive terms,* such as *"I think"*, *"I guess"*, *"I feel"*. If you use them excessively, they will negatively affect the impression you are trying to leave with the interviewer. Research indicates that women use these tentative terms more frequently than men. By using these indecisive terms, you can -- male or female -- appear indecisive and somewhat muddled. You want to communicate that you are a clear and purposeful individual.

Ninth, avoid the use of ambiguous and somewhat *negative terms* such as *"pretty good"* or *"fairly well"*. These terms say little if anything. They may even communicate negatives -- that what you did was not good!

Most people could improve their use of positive form. But it is difficult for someone to follow those suggestions after reading them the night before the interview. One needs to begin making the necessary changes well in advance of the interview. It can be done if one really wants to make the changes, but for most people it takes concerted effort over time. By all means, do not pass up the nine opportunities for using positive form in the interview.

ANALYZE YOUR LISTENER

Public speakers are always advised to analyze both their audience and their situation before speaking. The same advice should be followed when you interview. *The language you use should vary according to the interviewer.* If the interviewer is from the personnel office with little or no background in your field of expertise, your language should be less technical than it would be if you were talking with someone who shares your technical background. If you are interviewing with someone in your area of expertise, who also has the technical background, you should use a vocabulary relevant to the job in order to build common ground as well as your credibility. But don't overdo the use of jargon.

Analysis of your situation should tell you this is not the time for excessive modesty. Of course, you do not want to become an obnoxious braggart, but you do want to present your strengths -- skills and accomplishments -- in a positive way. Therefore, don't be reluctant to *talk about yourself and your accomplishments*. Remember, the interviewer wants to know more about you, especially your potential value to him or her. The more positive information you can communicate to the interviewer, the stronger your position will be in the final hiring decision.

A frequent question asked by prospective interviewers is *"How honest should I be?"* Most individuals have something in their background they believe would work against them in getting the job if the interviewer knew about it. They wonder if they should tell the interviewer before he or she finds out. We advise you to be honest -- but not stupid. In other words, if asked a direct question about the thing you hoped to hide, answer honestly, but emphasize positives. Under no circumstances should you volunteer your negatives or weaknesses.

Present your strengths -- skills
and accomplishments -- in
a positive way.

MANAGE QUESTIONS WITH POSITIVE CONTENT

The actual content of your answers should be stated in the positive. One example of this is the type of hobbies you communicate to employers. As John Molloy notes, many employers prefer *"active"* hobbies, such as swimming, tennis, golfing, or jogging, to more sedentary activities, such as reading and stamp collecting.

But the most important examples of positive content relate to managing the specific interview questions which are designed to probe your knowledge, abilities, motivations, strengths, and weaknesses. The employer's goal is somewhat negative in the interview; he or she wants to know why *not* to hire you. The major unstated question is *"What are your weaknesses?"* Several other questions may be asked to indirectly answer this major one.

You should always phrase your answers to questions in a positive manner that stresses your value. Avoid the use of such commonly used negatives as *"can't"*, *"didn't"*, and *"wouldn't"*. These terms direct listeners into negative avenues of thinking. They do not communicate optimism and enthusiasm -- two qualities you should demonstrate in the interview. Take, for example, two different answers to the following interview question.

QUESTION: *Why did you major in business administration?*

ANSWER 1: *That's real funny. I wanted to major in history, but my parents told me if they were footing the bills, I shouldn't be studying useless subjects. I tried political science, biology, and accounting but didn't like any of them. Business administration wasn't that difficult for me. I couldn't think of anything I like more -- except perhaps history. And it's not a bad field to be in these days.*

ANSWER 2: *I always enjoyed business and wanted to make it a career. As a youth I had my own paper route, sold books door to door, and was a member of Junior Achievement. In college I was involved in a couple of small businesses. It seems as though I have always been in business. I tend to have a knack for it, and I love it. My major in business administration further strengthened my desire to go into business. It gave me better direction. What I want is to work with a small and growing firm that would use my abilities to plan and implement marketing strategies.*

While the first answer may be the most truthful, it presents a negative and haphazard image of you. The second answer, while also truthful, stresses the positive by communicating strengths, purpose, and enthusiasm.

Let's take as another example an employer who asks the interviewee why he is leaving his present job:

QUESTION: *Why are you leaving your present job?*

ANSWER 1:   *After working there three years, I don't feel I'm going anywhere. Morale isn't very good, and the management doesn't reward us according to our productivity. I really don't like working there anymore.*

ANSWER 2:   *After working there three years, I have learned a great deal about managing people and developing new markets. But it is time for me to move on to a larger and more progressive organization where I can use my marketing experience in several different areas. I am ready to take on more responsibilities. This change will be a positive step in my professional growth.*

Again, the first answer communicates too many negatives. The second answer is positive and upbeat in its orientation toward skills, accomplishments, and the future.

Most interview questions can be answered by using positive language that further emphasizes that you are competent, intelligent, friendly, spontaneous, honest, and likeable. This language should project your strengths, purpose, and enthusiasm. If you feel you need to practice formulating positive responses to interview questions, examine the sample questions outlined earlier in this chapter. Consider alternative positive responses to each question. You also may want your spouse or friend to ask you interview questions. Tape record the interview and review your responses. Are your answers positive in both form and content? Do they communicate your strengths, purpose, and enthusiasm? Keep practicing the interview until you automatically respond with positive yet truthful answers.

OVERCOME OBJECTIONS AND NEGATIVES

Interviewers are likely to have certain objections to hiring you. Some of their objections may be legitimate whereas others are misunderstandings. Among these objections are questions relating to your bona fide qualifications -- education, experience, and skills.

If you are weak in any of the qualification areas, you may not be able to overcome the objections unless you acquire the necessary qualifications. But chances are these qualifications have been screened prior to the interview and thus will not be a topic of discussion. If, on the other hand, your education, experience, and skill level pose any objections in the mind of the interviewer, stress again your strengths in a positive and enthusiastic manner. Objections to your educational background will be the easiest to deal with if your experience and skills demonstrate your value.

On the other hand, one objection individuals increasingly encounter today from employers is being *over-qualified*. More and more people by choice are moving *down* in their careers rather than up. Given the desire for and ease of higher education, more and more people appear over-educated for many jobs today.

Employers' objections to candidates being over-qualified are a legitimate concern. From the perspective of employers, the over-qualified individual may quickly become a liability. Becoming unhappy with the job, they leave after a short period of time. Other individuals may have an unrealistic ambition of quickly moving up the organizational ladder. In either case, the over-qualified individual may cost an employer more than he or she is worth.

On the other hand, the over-qualified candidate may think he or she is doing the employer a favor -- the company is getting more for their money. If this is your perception of your value, you need to change it immediately. Unless you are prepared to take a position which is beneath your qualifications and can clearly communicate your desire to the employer so as to lessen his or her fears, you will most likely not get the job. In the interview you must convince the employer that you understand his or her apprehension about you, but you are willing, able, and eager to do the job.

While you want to communicate your strengths, employers want to know your weaknesses. There are several ways to handle questions that try to get at your weaknesses. If the interviewer frankly asks you *"What are some of your weaknesses?"*, be prepared to give him or her positive responses. You can do this in any of four different ways:

STRATEGIES FOR
HANDLING NEGATIVES

1. DISCUSS A NEGATIVE WHICH IS NOT RELATED TO THE JOB BEING CONSIDERED:

I don't enjoy accounting. I know it's important, but I find it boring. Even at home my wife takes care of our books. Marketing is what I like to do. Other people are much better at bookkeeping than I am. I'm glad this job doesn't involve any accounting!

2. DISCUSS A NEGATIVE WHICH THE INTERVIEWER ALREADY KNOWS:

I spent a great deal of time working on advanced degrees, as indicated in my resume, and thus I lack extensive work experience. However, I believe my education has prepared me well for this job. My leadership experience in college taught me how to work with people, organize, and solve problems. I write well and quickly. My research experience helped me analyze, synthesize, and develop strategies.

3. DISCUSS A NEGATIVE WHICH YOU MANAGED TO IMPROVE UPON:

I used to get over-committed and miss important dead-lines. But then I read a book on time management and learned what I was doing wrong. Within three weeks I reorganized my use of time and found I could meet my deadlines with little difficulty. The quality of my work also improved. Now I have time to work out at the gym each day. I'm doing more and feeling better at the same time.

4. DISCUSS A NEGATIVE THAT CAN ALSO BE A POSITIVE:

I'm somewhat of a workaholic. I love my work, but I sometimes neglect my family because of it. I've been going

> *into the office seven days a week, and I often put in 12 hour days. I'm now learning to better manage my time.*

TAKE INITIATIVE

Employment recruiters indicate that the most appealing candidates are those who take some initiative during the interview. We are not suggesting that you take control of the interview, but you need not play a completely passive role either. Taking initiative is a quality many employers prize in their employees. Indeed, many employers wish they could find more employees who would take initiative!

Even with the best interviewer, you will need to ask questions. Remember, you have a decision to make too. You need answers to some important questions about your future:

- Are you really interested in the job?

- Does it fit your goals and skills?

- Will it give you the chance to do something you do well and enjoy doing?

- Will it give you an opportunity to move in some of the directions you want to move?

Use the interview situation to get answers to these and other questions that are critical to your future. When you get to the final set of questions concerning compensation, you should be well prepared to negotiate a salary based upon knowledge of the value of both you and the position.

Chapter Eight

NEGOTIATE SALARY AND BENEFITS

While the salary question can arise anytime during a job interview, it is the central issue when you receive a job offer. In fact, you never accept a job offer until you have solved the issue of compensation. Put another way, the employer may say *"We are prepared to offer you the job as long as we can reach agreement on compensation."* At this point the nature of the interview shifts toward benefits *you* will receive from the organization in exchange for your talents. No longer must you be only employer-centered. It's time to be somewhat self-centered as you translate your value and the value of the position into dollars and cents.

This is not the time to be shy about money. You must address the compensation question head-on in as professional but earnest a manner as possible. For the salary figure you agree on at this time will largely set the stage for future salary increments which are likely to be figured as a percentage of your base salary. Your basic goal should be to negotiate the highest salary possible as an indication that you will offer excellent value to the employer and the organization. How you arrive at a mutually agreeable figure requires strong negotiation skills.

LEVELS OF FLEXIBILITY

Contrary to what some negotiation experts may tell you, not everything is negotiable. When it comes to salary and benefits, most employers have little flexibility to negotiate beyond very narrow ranges assigned to positions. Part of the reason is that most organizations have relatively rigid pay systems that are designed to be equitable and easy to administer. In many cases this rigidity is backed by laws designed to minimize discrimination based upon race, sex, and age. In part it is due to the fact that most positions are low to medium level positions – the ones least likely to be given salary flexibility.

Contrary to what negotiation experts may tell you, not everything is negotiable.

When we say not everything is negotiable, we primarily refer to levels of flexibility among various positions within organizations. Expect to find three levels of salary flexibility in most organizations based upon the level of the position within the organizational hierarchy. The general principle for negotiating salaries is this: higher level positions are the most negotiable; lower level positions are the least negotiable. Three levels of negotiations apply to different salary ranges:

- *Positions paying less than $20,000 a year:* Most of these positions are assigned a specific hourly or yearly salary figure. At this level employers need not negotiate salaries for several reasons: these are the most numerous positions with easily identified salary comparables found in the organization; many are entry-level positions; laws govern salary discrimination at this level; unions negotiate group contracts for many workers at this level; and an over-supply of candidates are available to fill these positions. As a result, the salary structure for these positions is the most rigid of any within most organizations. What flexibility exists may involve only a few hundred dollars of negotiating room -- a form of token negotiation -- or a flexible benefits package which is equitably administered throughout the organization.

- *Positions paying between $20,000 and $60,000 a year:* These mid-level positions may only constitute 20 percent of the total workforce within an organization. Most will be technical and professional positions which normally are assigned narrow salary ranges, depending on an individual's qualifications and experience. While employers have more flexibility to negotiate salaries in these pay ranges, pay systems still limit their degree of flexibility. Consequently, don't expect employers to be able to negotiate more than 15 percent above their stated salary figure. The stated range for many of these positions is between 10 and 20 percent. For example, a job paying 30,000 a year may have a salary range between $27,000 and $33,000. A $50,000 a year job may be assigned a range between $45,000 and $55,000. If you hope to go beyond a position's narrow salary range, you may need to focus your attention on redefining the position or creating a new position that has a higher salary range.

- *Positions paying more than $60,000 a year:* Employers usually have the most flexibility in negotiating salaries in the $60,000 plus range. These are normally top level management positions which require special skills and experience that are hard to find in the market place. In addition, recruiting for these positions may be quite different than recruiting for the mid and low-level positions. Employers, for example, may contract-out the hiring to specialized executive recruitment firms. Candidates, in turn, may use intermediaries to negotiate their compensation packages. It would not be unusual for someone offered a salary of $135,000 a year to negotiate a compensation package worth twice this figure. This big-bucks negotiating involves much more flexibility on the part of the employer who places much higher value on these positions than other positions in the organization. Since many of these positions are not part of the rigid pay system, they are *"open"* and fully *"negotiable"* when it comes to questions of salary and benefits.

Whatever you do, avoid approaching employers with the idea that salaries for all positions are negotiable. The principles of salary negotiation are disproportionately distributed to the fewest number of positions. Some salaries are negotiable, but many aren't. And many that are negotiable are only negotiable within very limited ranges. The degree to which a position is negotiable depends on the position, the employer, the' organization, and your perceived value. In other words, many positions are more or less negotiable depending on several factors. You will have some idea of the degree to which a position is negotiable once you discuss the issue of compensation, including the company's pay system, with the employer. This should occur prior to or during the salary negotiation session.

NEGOTIATING TECHNIQUES

Once you reach the negotiating stage and have some idea of the employer's degree of salary flexibility, you should be prepared to negotiate the highest salary possible. Here you have several negotiating techniques from which to choose. Most of these techniques are appropriate for positions in the $20,000 to $60,000 a year range as well as for individuals who negotiate their own salaries above $60,000 a year. If you use a salary negotiating intermediary, such as a professional headhunter or employment agency representative who has strong salary negotiating skills, you need not get involved in this negotiating scenario.

After identifying what salary the employer is likely to offer, as discussed in Chapter Seven, you have several choices on how to best approach the salary question. During the salary negotiation interview the employer will either ask you *"What are your salary requirements?"*, or identify what he or she is prepared to offer: *"We are prepared to offer you a salary of $37,000 a year. Would that be satisfactory?"* Each question should elicit a different response from you. In the case of the first question, you should not be the one to volunteer a salary figure. It is to your advantage to have the employer reveal what he or she is prepared to offer you. If you state your salary requirement first, you might state too high or too low a figure and thus give the salary advantage to the employer. If and when this question arises, try turning it around so the employer reveals the salary range earmarked for the position:

EMPLOYER: *What are your salary requirements?*

YOU: *If I remember correctly, this is the first time we've talked about the salary for this position. Could you tell me what the salary range is for this position as well as for someone with my qualifications?*

Unless the employer is playing a game with you, he or she should reveal the salary which is the amount budgeted for the position. Pause for a few seconds as you indicate nonverbally that you are thinking it over. By all means avoid looking overly enthusiastic or terribly disappointed. Remember, this is the time to negotiate a salary that should be either at the top of the employer's budgeted range, or beyond.

Once you know the employer's salary range, you should be prepared to do some hard but professional bargaining. At this point you can respond to the employer's salary range four different ways. First, you can indicate that the employer's figure is acceptable to you and thus conclude your final interview. Second, you can haggle for more money in the hope of reaching an acceptable compromise. Third, you can delay final action by asking for more time to consider the figure. Finally, you can tell the employer the figure is unacceptable and leave.

The first and the last options indicate you are either too eager or you are playing hard-to-get. We recommend the second and third options. If you decide to reach agreement on salary in this interview, haggle in a professional manner. You can do this best by establishing a *salary range* from which to bargain in relation to the employer's salary range. For example, if the employer indicates that he or she is prepared to offer $30,000 to $35,000, and these figures are consistent with the salary data you gathered from your research, you should immediately establish *common ground* for negotiation. You do this by stating your own salary range which overlaps the employer's range. For example, if the employer's range is $30,000 to $35,000, respond by saying:

> *Yes, that does come near what I was expecting. I'm thinking in terms of $35,000 to $40,000.*

You, in effect, *place the top of the employer's range into the bottom of your range.* By doing this you spread the range an additional $5,000 and put yourself into the high end. At this point you should be able to negotiate a final salary of $37,000 or $38,000, depending on how much flexibility the employer has with salaries or how willing he or she is in going to bat for you to justify a salary above the budgeted range. At the very least, assuming you have supported your qualifications, you have made it more likely that the employer will agree to $35,000 rather than try to get you for $30,000.

Most employers have more flexibility with salary ranges than they are willing to admit.

Most employers have more flexibility with salary ranges than they are willing to admit. They will find the money to hire you if they are convinced they are hiring top talent. Indeed, it would be foolish for them not to consider the fact that you will probably give them a much better return for their money than other candidates, especially when only a few hundred or thousand dollars separate you from a final agreement. And since the employer has already invested much time in you, unless there is a strong second candidate, it will probably cost the organization more than $1,000 to $2,000 to recruit someone else for this position.

Once you have placed your expectations at the top of the employer's salary range, you need to again emphasize your value.

Remember the supports we discussed in previous chapters. It is not enough to simply state you were *"thinking"* in a certain range; you must state *why* you believe you are worth what you want. Ideally, your explanation should be based on facts, centered around the employer's interests, and stress the benefits you will bring to the organization. You might say, for example,

> *The salary surveys I've read indicate that the salary for the position of _____in this industry and region is between $32,000 and $38,000. Since, as we have discussed, I have extensive experience in all the areas you outlined, I would not need training in the job duties themselves -- just a brief orientation to the operating procedures you use here at _____. I'm sure I could be up and running in this job within a week or two. Taking everything in consideration -- especially my skills and experience and what I see as my future contributions to your company -- I really feel a salary of $38,000 is fair compensation. Is this possible here at _____?*

---

*How you handle the salary
negotiation will affect
your future relations
with the employer.*

Always keep in mind that you should negotiate from a position of strength -- not greed. Establish your value, learn what the employer is willing to pay, keep your salary rationale employer-centered in stressing benefits, and negotiate in a professional manner. How you handle the salary negotiation will affect your future relations with the employer. In general, applicants who negotiate well will be treated well on the job.

HANDLING SALARY OBJECTIONS

While hopefully your salary negotiation session will go smoothly and you will quickly reach agreement with the employer, many employers will raise objections to candidate's stated salary requirements. When this happens, you must be prepared to handle these objections in a positive manner that once again stresses your qualifications and benefits for the employer. This is another opportunity to be redundant about qualifications, value, performance, and benefits. Whatever the objection, you must consistently talk about the importance of being rewarded for your performance. In so doing, you turn what are potentially negatives into positives that should further strengthen your position with the employer.

You can expect to encounter any, or all, of these three most common salary objections:

- *Your figure is not within our budget. We can't afford to pay that much for this position.*

- *Others with similar qualifications and experience don't make that much in our organization.*

- *Your salary history doesn't really justify such a large salary increase.*

All of these objections to your salary request are based upon rationale unrelated to your value or performance. For example, while a *budget* always seems to be a constraint when hiring new personnel, it should not be if you have demonstrated that the employer will get a high return from your performance. Communicate your value to employers in basic cost-benefit terms -- your special talents in exchange for higher performance and profits. You are an investment for greater profitability. Approaching the objection in this manner, respond to the employer by saying:

While I know you may have budgeted this position under $35,000, I also know many employers are willing to pay more than that. More importantly, I feel I bring to this position special skills, experience, and a commitment to performance that more than justify the $38,000.

The rationale that you will be *paid more than others* is another non-issue for you. This is the employer's problem – not your's. What the employer pays other employees is his or her business. Your concern is that you be fairly compensated for your performance. You might respond to the employer in this manner:

> *From what you told me earlier about the importance of reward-ing performance, I expected I would be offered a salary based upon my performance rather than one capped by what others make in the organization. In fact, this raises an issue that I need further clarification on: Exactly how will I be rewarded for my performance? Are raises largely a function of cost-of-living increases, or is the performance appraisal tied to yearly salary increases? I'm not sure if I understand how the compensation system operates in practice.*

The rationale that your *salary history* does not justify such a salary increase is another non-issue. You are not applying for a salary increase. Rather, you want to be compensated for the value of your work. Your salary history should have less bearing on what you receive in this position. You might respond this way:

> *I assumed I would be fairly compensated for my performance. I'm not sure how my past salary has any bearing on my work for you. In fact, I've carefully looked at this job in terms of duties and responsibilities as well as compared it to salaries in other organizations. I feel $38,000 is quite fair for what I've indicated I would achieve this first year. Would you agree that this is a fair way of arriving at this salary figure?*

As you continue to stress the performance issue in relation to compensation, you take the offensive as well as put the employer on the defensive. By taking the high road, which focuses on financially rewarding performance, you force the employer into explaining why compensation in this organization may not be related to performance. Few employers are comfortable justifying why they don't reward performance!

RECEIVING BENEFITS

Many employers will try to impress candidates with the benefits offered by the company. These might include retirement, bonuses, stock options, medical and life insurance, and cost-of-living adjustments. If the employer includes these benefits in the salary negotiations, do not be overly impressed unless they translate into significant income equivalents. While benefits are important, they mainly differ *among* employers; few are negotiable with a particular employer except for a key employees. Therefore, most benefits are standard -- they come with the job. When negotiating salary, it is best to talk about specific dollar figures.

On the other hand, if the salary offered by the employer does not meet your expectations, but you still want the job, you could try to negotiate for some benefits which are not considered standard. These might include longer paid vacations, some flextime, and profit sharing. If the employer offers a flexible benefit package, and you receive some of the same benefits via your working spouse's compensation package, find out if some benefits with this employer can be taken in cash.

Some of the most important benefits you need to review with the employer include the following checklist of items:

[ ] Health, disability, and life insurance
[ ] Reimbursement accounts
[ ] Supplementary pay plans
[ ] Education and training programs
[ ] Child and day-care services
[ ] Paid vacation time
[ ] Unpaid leave time
[ ] Retirement plans
[ ] Bonuses
[ ] Savings plans
[ ] Professional membership dues
[ ] Profit sharing plans
[ ] Cost-of-living adjustments
[ ] Relocation expenses
[ ] Perks (office, car, parking, equipment)
[ ] Termination agreement (severance pay)

Each of these benefits involves numerous additional issues, most of which are non-negotiable. Most companies attempt to offer and administer benefits equitably. In other words, everyone within the organization receives the same benefits regardless of their position or salary. The major differences arise when comparing the benefits of one company with those of another. The benefits package in one company, for example, may be equivalent to 35 percent of your base salary whereas in another company it may only be worth 15 percent of your salary. The differences are due to the number and extent of benefits offered by each company. For example, insurance programs with some employers involve full coverage whereas those with other employers require some employee contribution. Retirement programs with some companies offer early-out options and a limited vested period and thus greater portability than programs with other companies that require a lengthy vested period and limited portability. Reimbursement accounts, day-care services, and supplementary pay programs in one company may translate into a great deal of compensation for employees but these benefits may be absent in other companies.

On the other hand, some employers offer flexible benefits which present employees with *options*. These companies give employees a menu of benefit options from which to choose. If you are seeking employment with such a company, such benefit options will give you greater flexibility in structuring your total compensation package. During the salary negotiation session, be sure to inquire about such options.

RENEGOTIATE THE FUTURE

In some cases you may want a job which does not meet your immediate salary expectations. The employer may not be able to add on special benefits to satisfy you. When this happens, you might ask the employer during the interview to reconsider your salary after six months on the job. You request a six month performance review in which your salary will be reconsidered in light of your performance. Another approach is to ask the employer to consider expanding the job description or upgrading the position and salary. Such provisions would give you time to demonstrate your value. Employers have little to lose and much to gain by agreeing to such a provision. If other negotiating approaches fail, this one is at least worth trying. At least it stresses one of your major work values – you want to be rewarded for performance.

However, you should attempt this only as a last resort. In most cases, your strongest negotiating position is *before* you accept the job offer. Once hired, unless your performance is spectacular, you are less likely to receive more than the company's normal annual increments.

NEGOTIATING IN NON-NEGOTIABLE ENVIRONMENTS

Many jobs are found in organizations that do not negotiate salaries with individuals. The two major non-negotiable environments are government and companies where unions play an important role in determining compensation. In these situations, the question of salary and benefits is handled through a collective bargaining process or some other form of labor-management relations. Individuals join unions or professional groups that periodically address the compensation issue for the group as a whole. Wages and benefits are rigidly defined in order to be both equitably distributed and easily administered to everyone in the workforce. Salaries are normally assigned to qualifying levels, steps, or grades.

If you apply for a job with such an organization, you can expect to receive a salary and benefits assigned to the position as defined by the negotiated pay system. While individuals have little or no input into determining their salary and benefits in such systems, many individuals do manage to affect their compensation nonetheless. The major technique for negotiating in non-negotiable environments is to concentrate on the qualifications assigned to the position in order to upgrade the position. In the case of government, for example, salaries are graded according to the level of positions as defined by qualifications and experience. The lower the level of the position, the lower the salary. Therefore, if you want to move into the higher levels of the salary scale, you must have the qualifications and experience required for positions at those levels. Negotiating in this environment involves concentrating on the qualifications for positions.

You have two options here. First, you can *redefine your qualifications* so they meet the requirements of the higher-level positions. You do this by carefully analyzing the qualifications specified for the position as well as your own background. Try to match the two as closely as possible. If you are interested in working for the Federal government, for example, some agencies may even help you rewrite your SF-171 (the standard application form used in government) so it best meets the qualifications specified for the position. In so doing, you may receive a higher salary than you would have had you not had such agency assistance. The key to getting a high rating is how you describe your knowledge, skills, abilities, and other characteristics (KSAO factors).

In the second option, you might persuade the employer to *create a new position* which will be defined around your qualifications. Widely practiced in government and other organizations, this is called *"wiring"* a position. An employer who wants to hire a particular individual literally writes a new position description around the qualifications of the individual. The position is defined at the salary level, step, or grade that is acceptable to the candidate.

> *Many employers are reluctant to negotiate salaries upwards prior to seeing you perform in their organization.*

DON'T EXPECT TOO MUCH

Many applicants have unrealistic salary expectations and exaggerated notions of their worth to potential employers. Some occupational groups, such as postal and auto workers, appear overpaid for the type of skills they use and the quality of the work they produce. In recent years several unions began renegotiating contracts in a new direction -- downwards. Unions gave back salary increases and benefits won in previous years in order to maintain job security in the face of deepening recessions. Workers in many industries were not in a position to further increase their salaries. Many employers believed salaries had become extremely inflated in relation to profits. Such salaries, in turn, created even more inflated salary expectations among job hunters.

Given the declining power of unions, turbulent economic conditions, the increased prevalence of *"give-back"* schemes, and greater emphasis on productivity and performance in the workplace, many employers are reluctant to negotiate salaries upwards prior to seeing you perform in their organization. Especially in a tight job market, many employers feel they can maintain their ground on salary offers. After all, as more well qualified candidates glut the job market, many are willing to take lower salaries.

Given this situation, you may find it increasingly difficult to negotiate better salaries with employers. You will need to stress your value more than ever. You must communicate how you will benefit the employer. For example, if you think you are worth $35,000 a year, will you be productive enough to generate $300,000 of business for the company to justify that amount? If you can't translate your salary expectations into dollars and cents profits for the employer, perhaps you should not be negotiating at all!

Chapter Nine

FINALIZE THE OFFER

A job offer is not complete until you finalize the salary question. Once you reach a verbal agreement concerning compensation, you still need to do several things before starting the new job. How you handle this period may affect how well you get along on the job.

TAKE TIME

Once an employer offers you a job, you may want to ask for time to think it over. Ask to sleep on it for a day or two. A common professional courtesy is to give you at least 48 hours to consider an offer. During this time, you may want to carefully examine the job and consider other important questions at this stage:

- Is it worth what I am being offered?

- Can I do better?

- What are other employers offering for comparable positions?

If one or two other employers are considering you for a job, let this employer know his or her job is not the only one under consideration; you may be in demand elsewhere. This should give you a better bargaining position. Contact the other employers and let them know you have a job offer and that you would like to have your application status with them clarified before you make any decisions with the other employer. Depending on how much flexibility an employer may have to accelerate a hiring decision, you may be able to go back to the first employer with another job offer. With a second job offer in hand, you may greatly enhance your bargaining position.

With a second job offer in hand,
you may greatly enhance your
bargaining position.

CONSIDER THE OFFER

The job offer involves much more than a general invitation or commitment to hire you. If and when the employer says *"We want you to join our team"* or *"You're hired"*, you still need to work out the details of your employment. At the very least, these details should include four major components:

- Your specific duties and responsibilities.

- Expectations of your performance during the next year.

- A provision for reviewing both your performance and compensation.

- A compensation package.

You need to reach a mutual understanding about these important points that will affect your job. For example, both you and the employer should have a clear understanding of what exactly you will be doing in this job. Think of *duties and responsibilities* as your inputs into the company -- things you are expected to do on a day-to-day basis. If you don't know what your duties and responsibilities are, you may quickly discover the nature of the job changes. You may be expected to do many things you were never hired to do or things that have little to do with your strengths. Such a situation could become disastrous as you begin demonstrating your weaknesses rather than your strengths. Therefore, it's best to clarify your job duties and responsibilities at this point so that there will be no misunderstanding.

You also need to settle the issue of *performance*. What exactly are you expected to achieve during the first year? Does the employer have certain goals in mind for this position that can be clearly identified and measured? For example, are you expected to reorganize a section, increase markets and improve profits by a certain percentage, produce a certain number of reports, or represent the company at seven different meetings? Think of performance in terms of outputs or outcomes.

Think of performance in terms of outputs or outcomes.

Knowing your duties and responsibilities and understanding what performance is expected from you are only the first steps in completing the job offer. More importantly, you also need to know how performance is both *measured and rewarded*. For example, does the employer conduct annual performance reviews? If so, how are they conducted? What instruments are used? Does it involve a self-evaluation along with a peer and supervisory evaluation? What input will you have in the evaluation process? What other types of evaluations take place? For example, are nonproductivity evaluations used in determining raises and promotions?

At the same time, is the compensation system directly linked to the evaluation system? If the employer tells you that in this company performance is important and is rewarded, then the employer needs to spell out exactly how the system operates in practice. Ask for specifics. For example, when does the performance evaluation takes place? If the process begins in April, when does it conclude, and what final form does it take? Do you meet with your supervisor for feedback and for setting goals for the coming year, or is this an impersonal and secretive process just between your supervisor and his or her boss? Are raises and promotions largely a function of seniority or directly related to the performance evaluation?

These and other question should be answered prior to accepting any job offer. If not, these questions may soon arise on the job and the answers may well disappoint you. At that time, you will lament the fact that you did not seek clarification on how the employer's personnel and compensation systems operated.

> *Talk is cheap, and it often leads*
> *to misunderstandings if not*
> *put into writing.*

GET IT IN WRITING

Talk is cheap, and it often leads to misunderstandings if not put into writing. Questions of duties and responsibilities, expected performance, evaluations, and compensation lie at the heart of any job. These are important questions that require some form of written agreement and commitment on the part of the employer.

Verbal agreements may be okay between close and trusted friends, but they don't have much weight in employment situations. After all, the employer who made verbal agreements with you may be gone tomorrow, and he or she most likely will not share the commitments with the next employer. Verbal agreements that are important to you and your job should always be put into writing. You can start doing this by taking notes during the salary negotiation session. At some point, preferably near the end when you are expected to either accept or decline the offer, ask the employer to summarize your verbal agreement. As this is being done, write down each point. When he or see finishes summarizing the agreement, read back the agreement as you have written it down in your notes. And then finish by saying,

> *This is my understanding of what I will be expected to do as well as my compensation. Is this correct?*

Assuming the employer agrees, you should next ask if he or she could put this agreement in writing:

> *I would appreciate it if you could put this all in writing within the next two days. In addition to putting a copy in my personnel file, I would like a copy for my own files. I would appreciate if we would use this agreement as the basis for conducting a six month performance appraisal. I think this might be a good time to evaluate my work and to make sure we are going in the right direction with this job.*

If the employer has not been taking similar notes, make a copy for his or her reference. And make sure that the final written agreement indeed conforms to your notes and that it is completed within two days. You want this agreement in writing prior to quitting your present job and starting this new job.

ACCEPT, CLOSE, AND FOLLOW-THROUGH

Once you have a verbal agreement about the terms of your employment as well as an indication that your agreement will be put into writing within the next two days, you should accept the offer in both a professional and personal manner.

Assuming you have negotiated in a professional manner and both you and the employer are satisfied with the agreement, it is now time to set the stage for starting the job. At this point you want to make sure you are starting this job on the right foot. The employer now has certain performance expectations which are tied to the salary you negotiated. The employer will be carefully observing you over the next few months in hopes of confirming that he or she made the right hiring and compensation decisions. You do not want to disappoint the employer.

At the conclusion of the salary negotiation session, reassure the employer that he or she made the correct decision. You can do this by restating your interest in the job, your delight in joining the organization, and your commitment to performance. You want to express an important *attitude* here that should continue on the job. You might conclude by saying,

> *It's been a pleasure meeting and working with you on this position. I've been very impressed with the professional manner in which you have conducted the interviews and extended the job offer. I'm very much looking forward to joining you and your staff. This is the type of organization I believe is ideally suited for my long-term interests and skills. I'm very anxious to begin working on the new marketing plan for expanding our sales into Hong Kong and Taiwan. This is an area I've worked in for years, and I'm confident we will see some major progress here. Thank you for your trust.*

After leaving this session, you should follow-up your acceptance of the job offer with a nice thank-you letter in which you reiterate the same points you made at the conclusion of the salary negotiation session. This is a thoughtful and courteous thing to do. Employers tend to remember such thoughtful gestures in a positive manner. Such a letter may well set a very positive tone for future compensation discussions with this employer.

Job Offer Acceptance

7694 James Court
San Francisco, CA 94826
January 23, 19__

Judith Green
Vice President
West Coast Airlines
2400 Van Ness
San Francisco, CA 94829

Dear Ms. Greene:

I am pleased to be joining your organization and am looking forward to meeting you and your staff again next month.

The customer relations position is ideally suited to my background and interests. I assure you I will give you my best effort in making this an effective position within your company.

I understand I will begin work on February 21. If, in the meantime, I need to complete any paper work or take care of any other matters, please contact me.

I enjoyed meeting with you and your staff and appreciated the professional manner in which the hiring was conducted.

Sincerely,

Joan Kitner

Chapter Ten

SALARY INCREASES, RAISES, AND PROMOTIONS

Many of the principles we've outlined for dealing with the salary question during the job search are equally valid for negotiating salary increases once you are on the job. Some organizations conduct annual salary reviews whereas others deal with salaries and raises on an ad hoc basis. Depending on the type of organization you work for, you may be involved in an annual salary review process where a performance appraisal plays the central role in determining raises. On the other hand, you may work for an organization where raises are largely determined by annual cost-of-living increases as well as initiatives on the part of individual employees to negotiate higher salaries.

THE MYTH OF PERFORMANCE

Performance is important to employers and organizations. However, one must also be realistic about how performance is recognized, rewarded, and promoted. To just do a good job is not enough. You must communicate to others that you are a producer who gets things done for the group and organization.

At the same time, performance is one of those wonderful terms like efficiency and honesty. Almost everyone agrees it is important, but few do much about it. Many employers give lip service to performance but then reward people on the basis of seniority, inflation, and politics.

Just because employers say that performance is important in personnel decisions is no reason to believe they reward performance.

Performance is only one of many criteria for rewarding employees. It may or may not be the most important criterion compared to other on-the-job considerations. Therefore, if you want salary increases and promotions, you must understand how the personnel system operates in both theory and practice. It will vary from one organization to another. In some organizations it operates according to the book: rewards are dispensed through the operation of an objective performance appraisal system. In other organizations it operates according to Byzantine bureaucratic politics – the ebb and flow of power, influence, and intrigue. Whom you know and how you play the game of politics will largely determine your raises and promotions. Just because employers say that performance is important in personnel decisions is no reason to believe they reward performance. Unfortunately, you really won't know how it operates until you become part of the organization.

Indeed, it would be naive for us to suggest the reality of most organizations is that they put performance first. If they did, fewer companies would fail and most would do much better than they do at present. Most organizations are more or less performance oriented, depending on the internal structure of power and personnel. The reality is that you must work with people as well as with things and processes. While your performance may center around how well you work with things, your rewards will be dispensed by how well you work with the people who have power. Consequently, once on the job, you must take particular care of how well you deal with those who are important to your future. This may mean attaching yourself to a mentor who, in turn, sponsors you within the organization.

While all workers may enter the organization with similar qualifications and experience, those who get ahead do so because they do things differently from others. What they do different is much more than just performance. They also network their way to job and career success by being in the right place at the right time and with the right set of sponsors.

Focus on performance, but make sure it gets communicated to the right people who have the power to dispense rewards.

Nonetheless, your most important asset in getting ahead will be your performance. Focus on performance, but make sure it gets communicated to the right people who have the power to dispense rewards.

COMMUNICATE PERFORMANCE AND GET RAISES

Most employees receive raises on the basis of cost-of-living increases, performance criteria, bonuses, or promotions. Being incremental, most increases are figured as a percentage of one's present salary base -- 3 to 8 percent. Few employees receive major salary increases -- 10 to 30 percent -- other than those which come with promotions or major bonuses. In other words, they must change jobs within the organization in order to significantly boost their earnings. Therefore, your initial starting salary will be the major determiner of your future salaries with your present employer -- unless you do something different from other employees.

Ideally, everyone should be rewarded on the basis of their work performance. But in reality it is very difficult for employers to measure performance, because they often lack a performance appraisal system that would define jobs in terms of performance criteria. In addition, performance appraisals have a tendency to become politicized within organizations. They may create more internal conflicts and turmoil than they are worth. In the end, many employers prefer giving everyone across-the-board increases -- despite individual performance differences -- rather than get involved in the politics of performance appraisals. Principles of equity and ease of administration often over-ride such values as individual fairness when dealing with the issue of who gets how much of a raise this year. Not surprisingly, employers often lack a clear idea of what they want in a new employee since they have not tied performance criteria nor a performance appraisal system to the issue of compensation. Their preference for using salary history and comparative salary figures in justifying salaries is a further indication that they have not dealt with the critical issue of performance in the workplace.

If you work in an organization that uses an annual salary review process to determine raises, it's best to approach such a process the same way in which you would approach the salary negotiation when applying for a job. The key to making this process work in your favor is to *document* your performance. If a performance appraisal is central to the annual salary review, know what the performance criteria are and make sure you have been documenting your accomplishments throughout the year. In addition to the performance appraisal form used by the employer, you should keep a diary of your accomplishments. This might be in the form of a notebook in which you make entries at the end of each day or week. Include the following categories of information in your performance diary:

- *Achievements:* (those things that resulted in some type of improvement to my job or organization -- efficiency, effectiveness, profitability, etc.)

- **Problems solved:** (demonstrates your abilities and responsiveness to the needs of the organization)

- **New initiatives taken:** (documents initiative and added value to the organization)

- **Additional duties and responsibilities performed outside my job description:** (indicates an expansion of your job for which you should receive additional rewards).

Avoid the tendency to document *activities*, many of which are routines that produce few outcomes or accomplishments. You want to focus on those things that are more likely to be rewarded by employers – outcomes, results, or benefits.

In addition, you want to achieve a certain degree of *visibility* within the organization that communicates to your supervisor and his or her boss your value as well as your positive attitudes and behaviors. You do this through meetings, memos, and recognition through others. For example, you should keep your supervisor informed about what you are achieving. If you manage to acquire a new client or conclude a major sale, write a memo to your supervisor in which you document this achievement. If you receive recognition or praise from a customer or colleague relevant to your job, send a copy to your supervisor. When you attend meetings in which your supervisor is in attendance, make sure to contribute with intelligent questions and suggestions. As you continue to communicate value and performance to the employer, you want to build a reputation as someone who is good at what he or she does; you have the right attitude and you are reliable, trustworthy, and likeable. Such interpersonal communications should reinforce the written documentation you assemble in your performance diary as well as the information contained in your memos.

You should also *build networks* with mentors in the organization. Find successful people you admire and attach yourself to them for the purpose of better performing your job and learning how the organization operates. Ask them for advice on doing your job and moving up the organizational ladder. Let them know that you want to get ahead. While you want to be rewarded as a performer, you must also be realistic in terms of how rewards are dispensed within the organization. One of the best ways of getting your performance recognized and rewarded is to have a sponsor who takes a personal interest in seeing you move ahead.

***Find successful people you admire
and attach yourself to them.***

TAKING SALARY INITIATIVE

If you feel you are being under-compensated for your present level of work, you should do something about this problem. If you are not likely to be promoted to a higher paying job and salary raises are largely non-negotiable within your present organization, you might start looking for another employer. After all, your best salary will probably be the one you initially negotiate with a new employer. Begin conducting a job search but do so discretely. Avoid applying for jobs that appear to be blind ads. Your present employer could be behind since an ad, and it could be your position they are advertising! There is no better way of loosing your value in the eyes of your present employer than for him or her to find out that you are indiscretely looking for another job.

However, most employers have some flexibility to negotiate salary with their employees. Assuming you have gathered comparable salary data, documented your performance, and regularly communicated your performance to the employer, you should be in a strong position to talk with him or her frankly about your salary. Again, approach this issue from the employer's perspective rather than from a self-centered perspective of need or greed. If your needs are much above a salary that your present position can justify, you should focus your attention on a promotion rather than a salary raise; a new salary should automatically come with a new position. In addition to stressing your performance in your present job, you will need to convince the employer that you will also do well in a new position. Approach this discussion the same way you would a job interview. After all, you will be interviewing for a new job rather than just a salary raise. The difference is that the employer is already familiar with you as both a person and a professional.

> *Your best salary will probably*
> *be the one you negotiate*
> *with a new employer.*

When you speak with your employer about a raise or promotion, you should focus on why you deserve the money or position. Use supports to justify your request. Expect the employer to raise the same objections you would encounter during a job interview: budgetary limitations, company profits are down, the economy looks shaky, others don't make that much, and your salary history doesn't justify such an increase. Deal with these objections in the same manner as you would during the salary negotiation session of the job interview: focus on your value, but this time give examples of performance relevant to this employer and the organization.

THREATS AND ALTERNATIVE OFFERS

As a bargaining tool, threatening to quit unless your salary and promotion demands are met is a very risky, high stakes business. Never threaten to quit unless you really mean it. When given an ultimatum by an employee, many employers will thank the employee for his or her good work and then politely show them the door. Unless you are so instrumental to the functioning of the organization -- and few if any people are -- this negotiating tactic is likely to backfire.

You must be prepared to do what you say you will do. And that means having an alternative job offer in hand. Threatening to quit without such an offer is an invitation to self-induced unemployment!

On the other hand, if you have an alternative job offer, you should be in the strongest position to renegotiate your salary or discuss a promotion. Prepare a list of those things you would need in order to stay with this organization. Your discussion will be less focused on your performance than on what the employer needs to do in order to keep you. If the employer really wants you to stay, he or she should be able to find the money for a raise or the means to promote you.

If you unexpectedly submit your resignation, because you already accepted a job offer with another employer, your present employer may try to persuade you to stay by sweetening your compensation package as well as offering you a promotion. This is not a bad position to be in from the stand point of both employers. If your present employer offers you a deal you can't refuse, you might be better off staying where you are, since you have substantially increased your value in the eyes of this employer. On the other hand, the new employer might feel deceived, since it appears you used him or her as leverage for getting a promotion and raise. You might also go back to the new employer and share your new problem: your present employer is offering you a better position and compensation package than this employer. While sensitive and somewhat embarrassing for some people, this is the type of problem many employees wish they encountered more often. Just make sure you don't alienate both employers in the process of bargaining for a better position and more compensation. You could very well find yourself burning both ends of the candle while holding it in the middle!

Chapter Eleven

FIND YOUR
SALARY RANGE

Identifying salary ranges for particular jobs is relatively easy given numerous studies that survey salaries. However, the more you learn about salary ranges, the more elusive this information seems for particular situations and the less useful it becomes for individual decision-making. What we need to do is critically examine the nature of salary surveys and their relevance to your particular situation.

SALARIES AND SALARY RANGES

The basic problem with salary surveys is that most are conducted on a national or regional level for general types of positions, but individuals work in specific positions, for special organizations, within specific communities. While national and regional salary information may give you a general idea of the high and low salaries for certain types of jobs, they do so only in the aggregate. Furthermore, salary surveys tend to be inconsistent. We will use as an example salaries for accountants as we survey some of the information sources available to you. You can get similar information for many other occupations from these same sources. Most should be found in your local library.

According to the Bureau of Labor Statistics' study *White-Collar Pay: Private Service-Producing Industries, March 1989,* salaries for accountants fall into the following categories, averages, and ranges:

ANNUAL SALARIES

Occupation and Level	Mean	Median	Middle Range	
			First quartile	Second quartile
Accountants				
I	$22,073	$21,991	$19,992	$24,000
II	26,031	25,690	23,630	28,020
III	33,404	32,987	29,988	36,180
IV	43,304	42,637	39,184	46,981
V	54,627	54,203	48,980	59,754
VI	68,252	65,782	63,674	71,971
Chief Accountants				
II	55,196	54,978	50,980	60,000
III	72,156	71,471	66,972	76,469
IV	93,321	89,964	82,779	106,457
Auditors				
I	23,664	22,991	22,151	25,290
II	28,519	28,056	25,998	30,182
III	35,059	34,500	31,200	37,985
IV	43,384	42,368	39,708	46,981
Public Accountants				
I	25,335	25,000	23,990	26,700
II	27,505	26,989	25,490	29,488
III	31,390	30,648	28,189	33,786
IV	40,532	39,044	35,486	45,582

At the most general level, we can say according to the Bureau of Labor Statistics' study, accountants in 1989 made somewhere between $19,992 and $106,457. If you are applying for an entry-level accountant position, the national average for this type of position is $22,073 per year from a range of $19,992 to $24,000. We also know from this study that accountants in large organizations make more money than accountants in smaller firms:

AVERAGE (MEAN) SALARIES FOR
ACCOUNTANTS AND AUDITORS, 1989

Occupation and Level	Organizations with 50-999 workers	Organizations with 1,000-2,499 workers	Organizations with 2,500+ workers
Accountants			
I	$21,316	$22,142	$23,912
II	$25,338	$26,277	$28,458
III	$32,886	$33,273	$35,750
IV	$43,094	$42,225	$45,005
V	$53,681	$53,895	$56,393
Auditors			
I	$23,781	$22,967	$24,619
II	$27,515	$27,941	$29,860
III	$34,616	$33,880	$36,178
IV	$42,349	$42,193	$44,935

The Bureau of Labor Statistics also conducts *Area Wage Surveys* of all major metropolitan areas. These surveys can give you an overview of salary differences among metropolitan areas. Computer operators in San Francisco ($466.50 per week), for example, make a great deal more than computer operators in Tampa-St. Petersburg ($354.00 per week). Therefore, a national average salary figure would tell you little and perhaps mislead you about salaries in a particular community -- the most important information you need in order to deal with the salary question with a specific employer. You will find the average (mean) salaries and salary ranges for computer operators varies in the following 13 metropolitan areas:

AVERAGE SALARIES FOR COMPUTER OPERATORS, 1989

Weekly earnings (in dollars) Metropolitan area	Mean	Middle Range
Anaheim-Santa Ana, CA	434.50	381.00 - 498.00
Baltimore, MD	426.50	369.50 - 472.50
Chicago, IL	419.00	356.50 - 491.50
Dallas-Fort Worth, TX	410.50	338.00 - 465.00
Denver, CO	410.00	342.00 - 461.00
Houston, TX	430.50	344.00 - 496.00
Miami-Hialeah, FL	451.00	412.00 - 510.50
Minneapolis-St. Paul, MN/WI	396.50	350.00 - 429.50
New York, NY	457.00	400.00 - 518.50
Phoenix, AZ	408.00	351.00 - 458.00
San Francisco, CA	466.50	409.50 - 517.00
Tampa-St. Petersburg-Clearwater, FL	354.00	284.50 - 394.00
Wilmington, DE, NJ, MD	447.50	366.50 - 509.50

In smaller communities not included in this survey, you can expect earnings of computer operators to be significantly less.

Copies of these and other regional studies are available at all regional Bureau of Labor Statistics offices:

REGION I: **Connecticut, Maine, Massachusetts, New Hampshire, Rhode Island, Vermont**

> Kennedy Federal Building
> Suite 1603
> Boston, MA 02203
> Tel. 617/565-2327

REGION II: **New Jersey, New York, Puerto Rico, Virgin Islands**

Room 808
201 Varick Street
New York, NY 10014
Tel. 212/337-2400

REGION III: Delaware, District of Columbia, Maryland, Pennsylvania, Virginia, West Virginia

3535 Market Street
P.O. Box 13309
Philadelphia, PA 19101
Tel. 215/596-1154

REGION IV: Alabama, Florida, Georgia, Kentucky, Mississippi, North Carolina, South Carolina, Tennessee

Suite 540
1371 Peachtree St., NE
Atlanta, GA 30367
Tel. 404/347-4416

REGION V: Illinois, Indiana, Michigan, Minnesota, Ohio, Wisconsin

9th Floor, 230, S. Dearborn St.
Chicago, IL 60604
Tel. 312/353-1880

REGION IV: Arkansas, Louisiana, New Mexico, Oklahoma, Texas

Federal Building
525 Griffin Street, Rm. 221
Dallas, TX 75202
Tel. 214/767-6970

REGIONS VII AND VIII: Iowa, Kansas, Missouri, Nebraska (REGION VII); Colorado, Montana, North Dakota, South Dakota, Utah, Wyoming (REGION VIII)

Federal Office Building
911 Walnut St., 15th Floor
Kansas City, MO 64106
Tel. 816/426-2481

REGIONS IX AND X: Arizona, California, Hawaii, Nevada (Region IX); Alaska, Idaho, Oregon, Washington

71 Stevenson Street
P.O. Box 3766
San Francisco, CA 94119
Tel. 415/744-6600

The Department of Labor's *Occupational Outlook Handbook* also provides information on salaries and salary ranges. The 1990-1991 edition, for example, reports the following nationwide information on starting annual salaries for accountants as surveyed by the College Placement Council:

- Starting salaries for accountants
  with a BA degree: $25,300

- Starting salaries for inexperienced
  accountants with a master's degree: $28,800

- Beginning public accountants
  employed by public accounting
  firms: $22,100

- Nonsupervisory management
  accountants: $33,500

- Chief management accountants: $53,300

- Starting salary for junior
  accountants and auditors in
  the Federal government: $15,700

One especially useful piece of information found in the *Handbook* are the listings of professional associations for nearly 250 occupations that cover 101 million jobs or 86 percent of all jobs in the United States. As we noted earlier, many of these associations conduct their own annual salary surveys. Associations relevant to accountants, for example, include:

National Association of Accountants: 10 Paragon Drive, Montvale, NJ 07645

National Society of Public Accountants and the Accreditation: 1010 North Fairfax St., Alexandria, VA 22314

Other salary surveys also include information on accountants. However, many of these surveys use different categories of accountants that are noncomparative to other studies. The annual Robert Half *Salary Survey*, for example, provides salary range data on the following types of accountants for 1989:

Accountants -- Internal -- Large Firms (general, audit, cost):

0-1 years experience	$22,500 - $25,500
1-3 years experience	$24,000 - $31,000
Senior	$32,000 - $37,000
Management	$38,000 - $52,000

Accountants -- Public -- Large Firms (Audit, Tax, Management Services)

0-1 years experience	$23,000 - $26,000
1-3 years experience	$24,000 - $28,500
Senior	$29,000 - $33,000
Supervising Senior	$33,000 - $39,000
Manager	$40,000 - $62,000

Salary increases for accountants from 1989 to 1990 ranged from 4.2 to 6.7 percent. If you are interested in getting a copy of this survey, which also includes salary ranges in finance, banking, and information systems, contact the Robert Half office nearest you.

The 1990-1991 edition of Wright's *America Almanac of Jobs and Salaries* also includes information on salaries for accountants. However, the data is based upon the 1988 studies conducted by both the Department of Labor and Robert Half.

You need to think nationally but act locally when dealing with salaries and salary ranges.

FOCUS ON COMMUNITIES, ORGANIZATIONS, AND EMPLOYERS

While salary surveys provide you with useful nationwide and regional data, the problem with most studies is that they may not be relevant to your particular situation. You will have to take these studies one or two levels further as you focus on particular communities, organizations, and employers. In other words, you need to think nationally but act locally when dealing with salary and salary ranges. Examine these salary surveys for general guidelines, but do not take them as accurate reflections of the salary structure for positions in your community or the organization you are applying to or in which you work at present. To get accurate information on salaries at this level, you will have to conduct your own salary survey as we outlined in Chapter Four.

CONTINUING SALARY SUCCESS

Whatever you do, make sure you combine your qualifications and salary negotiation skills with a knowledge of salaries and salary ranges. The skills and resources we have outlined in this book should prepare you for the critical salary negotiation session with employers. If you engage in the data gathering and skill building we've suggested, you should be well prepared to achieve salary success both during the job search as well as on the job. The result should be thousands of dollars in additional income over the coming years. Better still, employers will assign higher value to you than to other employees who are less oriented toward translating their performance into higher salaries.

INDEX

CAREER RESOURCES

Call or write IMPACT PUBLICATIONS to receive a free copy of their latest comprehensive, illustrated, and annotated catalog of nearly 1,000 career resources.

The following career resources are available directly from Impact Publications. Complete the following form or list the titles, include postage (see formula at the end), enclose payment, and send your order to:

> **IMPACT PUBLICATIONS**
> 4580 Sunshine Court
> Woodbridge, VA 22192
> Tel. 703/361-7300
> FAX 703/335-9486

Orders from individuals must be prepaid by check, moneyorder, Visa or MasterCard number. We accept telephone and FAX orders with a Visa or MasterCard number.

Qty.	TITLES	Price	TOTAL

JOB SEARCH STRATEGIES AND TACTICS

Qty.	TITLES	Price	TOTAL
__	Careering and Re-Careering for the 1990s	$12.95	___
__	Complete Job Search Handbook	$12.95	___
__	Getting Hired	$9.95	___
__	Go Hire Yourself an Employer	$9.95	___
__	Joyce Lane Kennedy's Career Book	$29.95	___
__	The Right Place at the Right Time	$11.95	___
__	Super Job Search	$24.95	___
__	Wishcraft	$7.95	___
__	Who's Hiring Who	$10.95	___
__	Work in the NEW Economy	$14.95	___

SKILLS IDENTIFICATION, TESTING, AND SELF-ASSESSMENT

__ Charting Your Goals	$12.95	_____
__ Discover the Right Job for You!	$11.95	_____
__ Discover What You're Best At	$11.95	_____
__ Quick Job Hunting Map	$3.95	_____
__ Truth About You	$11.95	_____
__ What Color Is Your Parachute?	$17.95	_____
__ Where Do I Go From Here With My Life?	$11.95	_____

RESEARCH ON CITIES, FIELDS, AND ORGANIZATIONS

__ American Almanac of Jobs and Salaries	$15.95	_____
__ California	$9.95	_____
__ Career Finder	$9.95	_____
__ Careers Encyclopedia	$29.95	_____
__ Dictionary of Occupational Titles	$32.95	_____
__ Encyclopedia of Careers and Vocational Guidance (4 vols.)	$139.95	_____
__ *"How to Get a Job in..."* Atlanta, Chicago, Dallas/ Ft. Worth, Houston, Los Angeles/San Diego, New York, San Francisco, Seattle/Portland, Washington, DC ($15.95 or $139.95 for set of 9)	$139.95	_____
__ *Job Bank Series:* Atlanta, Boston, Chicago, Dallas, Denver, Detroit, Florida, Houston, Los Angeles, Minneapolis, New York, Ohio, Philadelphia, San Francisco, Seattle, St. Louis, Washington, DC ($13.95 each or $229.95 for set of 17)	$229.95	_____
__ Jobs Rated Almanac	$14.95	_____
__ Occupational Outlook Handbook	$24.95	_____

RESUMES, LETTERS, AND NETWORKING

__ Damn Good Resume Guide	$7.95	_____
__ Does Your Resume Wear Apron Strings?	$7.95	_____
__ Does Your Resume Wear Blue Jeans?	$7.95	_____
__ High Impact Resumes and Letters	$12.95	_____
__ Is Your *"Net"* Working?	$22.95	_____
__ Network Your Way to Job and Career Success	$11.95	_____
__ Perfect Cover Letter	$11.95	_____
__ Perfect Resume	$11.95	_____
__ Resume Catalog	$13.95	_____
__ Resumes That Knock 'Em Dead	$9.95	_____
__ Your First Resume	$10.95	_____

DRESS, APPEARANCE, AND IMAGE

__ Color Me Beautiful	$17.95	_____

__	Color Wonderful	$10.95	_____
__	Dress for Success	$9.95	_____
__	Professional Image	$10.95	_____
__	Winner's Style	$11.95	_____
__	Women's Dress for Success	$8.95	_____
__	Working Wardrobe	$11.95	_____

INTERVIEWS AND SALARY NEGOTIATIONS

__	Five Minute Interview	$12.95	_____
__	How to Make $1,000 a Minute	$8.95	_____
__	Interview for Success	$11.95	_____
__	Salary Success	$11.95	_____
__	Sweaty Palms	$10.95	_____

PUBLIC-ORIENTED CAREERS

__	American Almanac of Government Jobs and Careers	$14.95	_____
__	Compleat Guide to Finding Jobs in Government	$14.95	_____
__	Complete Guide to Public Employment	$15.95	_____
__	Directory of Executive Recruiters	$34.95	_____
__	Find a Federal Job Fast!	$9.95	_____
__	How to Get a Federal Job	$15.00	_____

INTERNATIONAL AND OVERSEAS JOBS

__	Complete Guide to International Jobs and Careers	$13.95	_____
__	Guide to Careers in World Affairs	$11.95	_____
__	How to Get a Job Overseas	$8.95	_____
__	International Careers	$11.95	_____
__	International Jobs	$12.95	_____
__	Overseas List	$13.95	_____

MILITARY

__	Re-Entry	$13.95	_____
__	Retiring From the Military	$18.95	_____
__	Woman's Guide to Military Service	$10.95	_____
__	Young Person's Guide to the Military	$9.95	_____

WOMEN AND SPOUSES

__	Careers for Women Without College	$10.95	_____
__	Relocating Spouse's Guide to Employment	$12.95	_____

COLLEGE STUDENTS

__	After College	$11.95	_____
__	College Majors and Careers	$16.95	_____
__	Internships	$24.95	_____
__	Liberal Arts Jobs	$11.95	_____

JOB LISTINGS

_ Federal Career Opportunities (6 issues)	$37.00	_____
_ Federal Jobs Digest (6 issues)	$29.00	
_ International Employment Hotline (12 issues)	$29.00	_____

CHILDREN, YOUTH, AND SUMMER JOBS

_ It's Your Future	$11.95	_____
_ A Real Job for You	$9.95	
_ Teenager's Guide to the Best Summer Opportunities	$9.95	

MINORITIES, IMMIGRANTS, DISABLED

_ Black Woman's Career Guide	$14.95	_____
_ Directory of Special Programs for		
Minority Group Members	$34.95	_____
_ Finding A Job in the U.S.	$8.95	_____
_ Job Hunting For the Disabled	$10.95	_____

EXPERIENCED AND ELDERLY

_ 40+ Job Hunting Guide	$10.95	_____
_ Getting a Job After 50	$29.95	_____
_ What's Next?	$11.95	_____

ALTERNATIVE CAREER FIELDS

_ Business and Management Jobs	$21.95	_____
_ Career Opportunities in the Music Industry	$27.95	_____
_ Careers in Engineering	$16.95	_____
_ Careers With Robots	$26.95	_____
_ Engineering, Science, and Computer Jobs	$23.95	_____
_ Flying High in Travel	$14.95	_____
_ Making It in the Media Professions	$18.95	_____
_ New Accountant Careers	$13.95	_____
_ *"Opportunities in..."* **Series** (125 titles: $12.95		
each or $1699.95 set; contact publisher)	$1699.95	
_ Outdoor Career Guide	$20.95	_____
_ Planning Your Medical Career	$17.95	_____

SUBTOTAL		_____
Virginia residents add 4.5% sales tax		_____
POSTAGE/HANDLING ($3.00 for first title and $.50 for each additional book)		_$3.00_
TOTAL ENCLOSED		_____